ARRO
COV
AND BUTE

C000230405

## 25 WALKS

# ARROCHAR, COWAL AND BUTE

## Alan Forbes

Series Editor: Roger Smith

**EDINBURGH : THE STATIONERY OFFICE**

© The Stationery Office 1997

First published 1997

Applications for reproduction should be made to The Stationery Office

### Acknowledgements

Firstly, I wish to thank Gregor Roy, of Bookpoint in Dunoon. It was Gregor
who first suggested to the publishers that thre should be a
25 Walks book for this area.
I also wish to thank the following for giving important information and
advice for this book: Kirsti (sic) Reid, formerly of Argyll & Bute Countryside
Trust, who is now involved in running the Achnamara-based environmental
consultants, Selkie Associates; Ian Everard of Forest Enterprise at Kilmun;
Anne Craig of Glendaruel Caravan Park; Suilven Strachan of Portavadie and
The Scottish Rights of Way Society.

British Library Cataloguing in Publication Data

A catalogue record for this book is available from the British Library

ISBN   0 11 495752 5

# CONTENTS

# USEFUL INFORMATION

The length of each walk is given in kilometres and miles, but within the text measurements are metric for simplicity. The walks are described in detail and are supported by accompanying maps (study them before you start the walk), so there is little likelihood of getting lost, but if you want a back-up you will find the 1:25 000 Pathfinder Ordnance Survey maps on sale locally.

Every care has been taken to make the descriptions and maps as accurate as possible, but the author and publishers can accept no responsibility for errors, however caused. The Countryside is always changing and there will inevitably be alterations to some aspects of these walks as time goes by. The publishers and author would be happy to receive comments and suggested alterations for future editions of the book.

## General Information
Tourist Information Centres at 7 Alexandra Parade, Dunoon, Argyll PA23 8AF. Tel 01396 703785; and 15 Victoria Street, Rothesay, Isle of Bute, PA20 0JA. Tel 01700 502151.

Information about Argyll Forest Park and its walks from Forestry Commission at Kilmun, by Dunoon, Argyll, PA23 8SE. Tel 01396 84666.

## Ferry Operators
Caledonian MacBrayne, the Ferry Terminal, Gourock, PA19 1QP. Tel 01475 650100.

Western Ferries, Hunter's Quay, Dunoon,PA23 8HJ. Tel 01369 704452.

## METRIC MEASUREMENTS

At the beginning of each walk, the distance is given in miles and kilometres. Within the text, all measurements are metric for simplicity (and indeed our Ordnance Survey maps are now all metric). However, it was felt that a conversion table might be useful to those readers who still tend to think in Imperial terms.

The basic statistic to remember is that one kilometre is five-eighths of a mile. Half a mile is equivalent to 800 metres and a quarter-mile is 400 metres. Below that distance, yards and metres are little different in practical terms.

| km | miles |
|----|-------|
| 1 | 0.625 |
| 1.6 | 1 |
| 2 | 1.25 |
| 3 | 1.875 |
| 3.2 | 2 |
| 4 | 2.5 |
| 4.8 | 3 |
| 5 | 3.125 |
| 6 | 3.75 |
| 6.4 | 4 |
| 7 | 4.375 |
| 8 | 5 |
| 9 | 5.625 |
| 10 | 6.25 |
| 16 | 10 |

# INTRODUCTION

More than 1,700 years ago Argyll, the Coastland of the Gaels, was invaded by the Scotti from Northern Ireland, who went on to occupy what is now Arrochar, Cowal and Bute. Today, however, many Scots explore the fondly named Arrochar Alps, but never discover the wonderful walks in the other two areas. This book attempts to restore the balance by highlighting some of the best walks in Cowal and on the Island of Bute, while not forgetting old favourites around Arrochar.

Dunoon and Rothesay still enjoy much of the popularity they had from Victorian times when steamers first brought thousands of holidaymakers "doon the watter" from the Glasgow area. But their beautiful hinterlands remain largely untouched and unpublicised compared to other parts of the Highlands.

This situation will not last much longer. When the last parking space in the farthest flung layby on Loch Lomondside remains occupied by somebody else's car, then walkers will look around for new places to explore. Cowal and Bute, so near yet so seemingly far off the beaten track are bound to be discovered afresh.

Walkers will discover a land which has been influenced by the sea and beautiful sea lochs which have cut into its coastline. It was the sea which brought the Scotti from Ireland to Argyll where they established their kingdom of Dalriada, and later conquered the Picts and unified Scotland.

The sea brought earlier neolithic settlers, the Vikings, the tourists and the US and Royal Navies, with their nuclear submarines. The sea has been such an influence on Cowal and Bute that if most of the photographs in this book show water in some form or another, I make no apology.

Four of the walks in this book follow the shoreline of lochs. Others follow burns up into hillsides or gorges. The great majority of walks are not long and present no real challenge in terms of navigation of difficult terrain.

Anyone wishing to try something more ambitious might try the Arrochar Alps walks at the start of the book, namely Cruach Tairbeirt, Beinn Narnain or the Brack. These are relatively serious walks and require an ability to use map and compass.

The weather in Argyll and Bute tends to be mild but `excessively humid' as one Victorian gazetteer euphemistically stated. Carry waterproofs but don't be surprised to encounter lots of sunshine, especially in spring, early summer and in autumn.

Lastly, it is worth knowing how one should deal with an unwanted travelling companion: the sheep tick. This tiny parasite breeds profusely in bracken where it can be brushed on to clothing. Ticks are occasionally the source of Lyme disease, an infection which can cause arthritis and heart disorders.

Although there is no need to get alarmed about this menace, it is useful to know how to avoid it. Ticks are most active from March to September, particularly May-June. This is the time when wearing shorts is popular, but long, close-weaved trousers are recommended to keep ticks away from the skin.

According to Professor Norman Grist, of the Scottish Centre for Infection and Environmental Health at Ruchill Hospital in Glasgow, the risk of infection is negligible unless the tick has been attached for more than 24 hours. A body inspection is recommended after every walk.

Popular methods of removal, such as applying alcohol, grease or a lighted match, is no longer recommended as it may provoke the tick to regurgitate infected fluid into the wound. Instead, a forceps should be used to grasp the mouth parts, and then gently pull while twisting slightly. Any fragment of tick left in the wound should be scraped out and the wound disinfected.

It has been a great pleasure searching out these 25 walks and I am sure that readers of the book will enjoy them every bit as much as I have.

Alan Forbes

*Opposite:* Looking to Lochgoilhead from the top of the Sruth Ban waterfall.

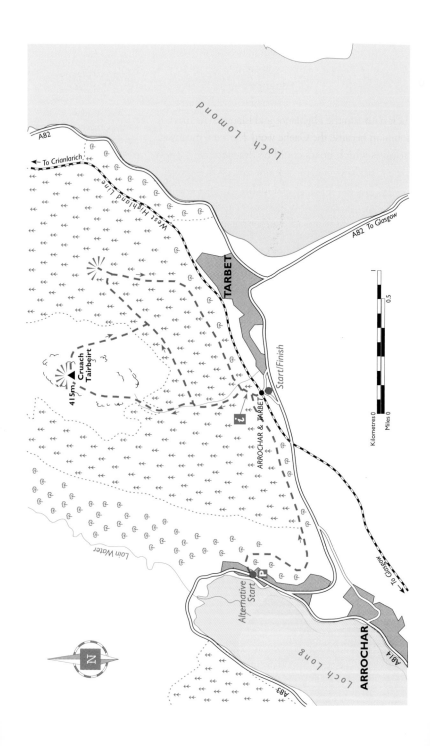

# CRUACH TAIRBEIRT

I f you ever arrange to meet someone at Tarbet, make sure that both of you are talking about the same place. The Ordnance Survey lists three Tarbets, four Tarberts and two places with Tarbat in their names in the Highlands and Islands. The name is common because the Gaelic word *Tairbeart* means an isthmus which boats could be dragged over. Such narrow necks of land are not uncommon in a country heavily indented by sea and lochs. This walk leaves the village of Tarbet on the western shore of Loch Lomond to climb Cruach Tairbeirt, the *hill or stack of the isthmus.*

The isthmus in question is the 2km neck of land separating Tarbet from Arrochar, at the northern end of Loch Long. It was over this short distance in 1263 that King Haakon of Norway's son-in-law Magnus dragged his galleys to raid settlements on Loch Lomond, who understandably were not expecting invaders in warships.

Cruach Tairbeirt is one of those hills which disprove the idea that the highest point gives the best view. The summit is only 415m (1,364ft) high, less than half the height of Ben Lomond on the opposite shore, yet it is possibly the best viewpoint of all the local hills in the Arrochar area.

Walkers can follow a circuit on a good path below Cruach Tairbeirt or enjoy most of the circuit while making a more strenuous detour to the summit. The walk begins at Arrochar & Tarbet Railway Station, but cars must not be parked there. Walkers can also park at Arrochar and take a good path through the woods to the station.

From the station, go under the railway line then uphill, through a gate and past an information board erected by the Friends of Loch Lomond and Forest Enterprise. Turn right where the path from Arrochar joins the route and continue to where the circuit path

## INFORMATION

**Distance:** Circuit path 2km (1.2 miles). Arrochar start adds 1.5km (1 mile) each way. Cruach Tairbeirt ascent adds a further1km.

**Start and finish:** Arrochar & Tarbet Station, at Tarbet, or public car park at Arrochar. *Do not park at station.* Spaces available at Black Sheep restaurant and craft shop near station.

**Terrain:** Good walking surface on circuit walk. Steep and tussocky summit climb requires stout walking shoes or boots.

**Public transport:** Arrochar & Tarbet station is on the West Highland Line from Glasgow. Scottish Citylink coaches on Glasgow-Oban/Campbeltown services pass the start.

**Refreshments:** Good choice in Tarbet and Arrochar.

soon splits. The right branch crosses a stream and runs east, above the railway line. The left branch follows the stream uphill.

To climb Cruach Tairbeirt, follow the left branch about 300m uphill until it crosses the stream. Leave the path and follow the stream uphill for about 100m, then branch right through a tunnel-like gap in the trees.

Heading up through the woods to the first viewpoint.

Light at the end of this tunnel leads you onto the open hillside. Here, a short, stiff pull over heather-clad slopes and hummocks takes you to the summit, crowned by a freshly-painted triangulation pillar, or trig point. The view from here really is outstanding: to the west, for instance, is the weirdly-shaped Cobbler and Loch Sloy Dam, and to the east you can see almost the full length of Loch Lomond.

An obvious track takes you down the eastern flank of Cruach Tairbeirt, overlooking Loch Lomond. This, of course, can also be used for ascent, but whichever

Cruach Tairbeirt from the shore of Loch Lomond.

direction you go, take care on a steep section below the summit plateau. The path leads to a gravel track which rejoins the circuit path on a bend, with green posts on either side of this junction. The summit should be climbed in clear weather, obviously because of the view but also to avoid confusion in finding your way back down.

To walk the circuit, follow the right-hand branch path after the information board. After a stand of silver birch you can look south down Loch Lomond. The path twice goes through a stone dyke then rises up, passing the lower edge of a plantation a couple of times. Cross a new bridge over a burn and head uphill between larches, with the burn below to your left.

Just before another new bridge, take a right fork at a viewpoint sign. A track leads through a firebreak split by a clump of trees. Take the right fork to reach a tussocky shoulder which is the viewpoint. The trees are so tall that you have to go to the end of the shoulder to see the loch and the mountains, particularly Ben Lomond.

Return to the path, turn right, and head back westwards along a pleasant, level stretch. The path eventually passes the two green posts on the bend, where the descent track from Cruach Tairbeirt meets the circuit path. The track can, of course, be followed uphill for a more open view over Loch Lomond.

Back at the circuit path, turn right again and continue to a clearing where you can rest on a bench looking south down the loch. The path continues to wend its way along to the stream, where the ascent of Cruach Tairbeirt begins. The path then descends steeply towards the station.

Sun setting on Loch Lomond.

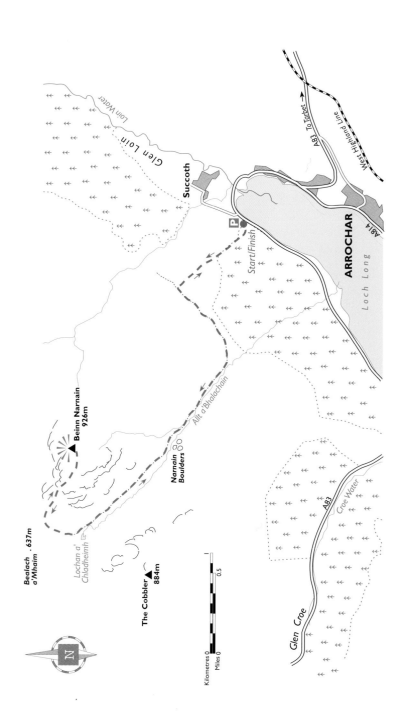

Loin Water

Glen Loin

Succoth

ARROCHAR

A814

Loch Long

West Highland Line

A83 To Tarbet

Start/Finish

Allt a'Bhalachain

Beinn Narnain
926m

Narnain
Boulders

Bealach
a'Mhaim . 637m

Lochan a'
Chladheimh

The Cobbler
884m

Glen Croe

A83

Croe Water

Kilometres 0 — 1
Miles 0 — 0.5

N

# BEINN NARNAIN

Mountains which dominate their neighbours tend to be described as *dramatic* or *noble* or *awe-inspiring*. Rarely are they described as being *bizarre* or *surreal*.

A mountain which is outlandish in more ways than one, however, is Ben Arthur, better known as The Cobbler. The weird summit, with a central ridge flanked by devil's horns, would do credit to Salvador Dali and anyone seeing it for the first time as they turn the corner into Arrochar never forgets that first impression.

At the risk of sounding contrary, this walk bypasses the Cobbler and heads for the summit of its nearest neighbour, Beinn Narnain. This is a higher but more retiring hill which offers an easier ascent, avoiding the sheer drops that can be encountered on The Cobbler. The reason for referring to The Cobbler, however, is that this is the hill that will command your attention for most of the ascent.

## INFORMATION

**Distance:** 10km (6 miles). Ascent: 900 metres (3000 ft).

**Start and finish:** Head of Loch Long, new walkers' car park on A83 road 2km from Arrochar.

**Terrain:** Hill paths, ranging from flat and well surfaced to steep, boggy and badly rutted. Grassy slope and small boulder field leading to summit. Walking shoes or boots needed.

**Public transport:** Scottish Citylink coaches to Arrochar on Glasgow-Oban/Campbeltown services. West Highland Line rail services from Glasgow to Arrochar & Tarbet Station, Tarbet.

**Refreshments:** Pubs and cafes in Arrochar and Tarbet.

The Cobbler looms over the route to Beinn Narnain.

The walk begins at the head of Loch Long, where there is a large new car park on the A83 road for the growing number of walkers who head for the 'Arrochar Alps', as this group of hills is affectionately called. Opposite the car park, a track leads into the woods beside an Argyll Forest Park sign. The track goes steadily uphill, following the concrete bases of an old railway line built to carry material for the construction of Loch Sloy dam nearby. This route goes through a plantation for a few hundred metres before coming out into the open. Below is a view of Arrochar village and over to the south is Cruach Tairbeirt (Walk 1).

Continuing steeply uphill, you come to a forestry road running across the hillside. Cross this road and rejoin the track heading uphill. The track is now badly eroded in parts and braids out at several points where walkers have tried to avoid the worst of the mud. You reach a different track which cuts across the lower slopes of Beinn Narnain. Above this junction is a larger concrete base marking the end of the line. Turn left and head west along the new track, which is level and well surfaced. Below, Loch Long stretches into the distance.

The track eventually swings round to the north-west past a small dam and there, up above, you see the crags of The Cobbler. Different explanations have been given for its name, but one possibility is that from some angles, the summit can look like a cobbler bending over his last. It is said that in the past the local Gaelic name for the peak was An Greasaiche Crom, which means 'the crooked shoemaker'.

The track follows the Allt a' Bhalachain (*Buttermilk Burn*) for about 1.5km up to its source, the Lochan a' Chladheimh, in the pass between The Cobbler and Beinn Narnain. Along this stretch the path leapfrogs streams flowing into the burn and passes through boggy stretches, but these obstacles can often be fun to cross.

About halfway up the burn are huge boulders which have a famous place in Scottish mountaineering history. These are the Narnain Boulders, which have been a shelter or *howff* for generations of climbers getting their first taste of rock climbing on The Cobbler. Beinn Narnain also has rock routes, but they are tucked out of sight, round to the right on Spearhead Ridge.

As you climb to the lochan, keep to the right of the burn. Continue past the lochan towards the Bealach a' Mhaim. *Bealach* is the Gaelic word for pass, and you are standing at a pass which is virtually a crossroads giving access not only to The Cobbler and Beinn Narnain but also to Beinn Ime, the tallest Arrochar Alp, ahead of you. Between Beinn Narnain and Beinn Ime is Coiregrogain, an outstanding example of a glaciated valley, which descends to the north-east.

At the bealach you almost double back to climb the grassy slope to Beinn Narnain's summit plateau. The

Looking over to Ben Lomond from the summit plateau of Beinn Narnain.

climb is easy, if taken steadily, but do not trend too far left otherwise you will miss seeing The Cobbler and you will get too close to a sheer gully on Beinn Narnain's northern slope.

A small boulder field has to be crossed before you reach the plateau, but this is no problem if you take care. On the plateau, a row of cairns leads to the triangulation pillar at the very top. From here there is a clear view of Ben Lomond, and a few yards away, the plateau ends at the edge of steep rock buttresses. A track does wend its way down through these cliffs, but it is not advised for the inexperienced or in mist.

Generally speaking, this hill should not be tackled in bad visibility because straying from the grassy ascent/descent slope could be hazardous. Return to the car park by the same route as used in the ascent.

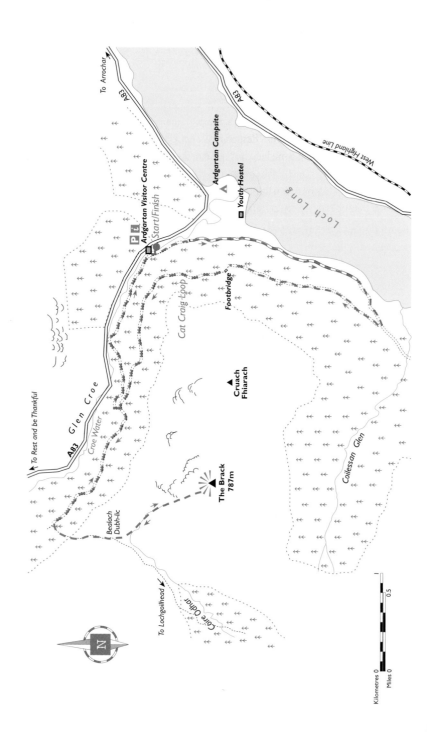

# THE BRACK

It is 1748, only two years since the Jacobites have been crushed at Culloden, and a regiment of redcoats are struggling to build a road over a mountain pass. At the top, some soldiers erect a stone inscribed with  words which will later sum up for many the rigours of Highland travel: *'Rest and Be Thankful'*. Today, the stone is long gone but the Rest remains as a picnic spot overlooking the old military road constructed by Major William Caulfeild's troops through Glen Croe and on to Inveraray.

This walk follows forestry roads, hugging the slopes of The Brack on the southern flank of Glen Croe. There are views up to the Rest, down to the military road and its successor, the less arduous A83, and across to the steep slopes of The Cobbler, or Ben Arthur.

Walkers have the choice of following the Cat Craig Loop, an 8km circuit starting and ending at Forest Enterprise's Ardgartan visitor centre beside the A83, or extending this route by climbing The Brack. The latter choice guarantees outstanding mountain views, but should only be tackled by the fit in good weather.

## INFORMATION

**Distance:** Distance: 8km (5 miles) for Cat Craig Loop plus 6km (3.5 miles) return to climb The Brack. Over 700m (2300ft) ascent to summit of The Brack.

**Start and finish:** Forest Enterprise visitor centre, Ardgartan, near Arrochar.

**Terrain:** Good roads and paths on Cat Craig Loop. The Brack is much more serious, on steep, rugged terrain requiring walking boots, waterproofs, food and drink, map (OS Landranger sheet 56) and compass.

**Public transport:** Scottish Citylink bus service runs through Arrochar on Glasgow-Oban/Campbeltown services.

**Refreshments:** Hotels and cafes at Arrochar and Tarbet.

The start of the walk at Ardgartan visitor centre.

From the visitor centre, cross the bridge over the Croe Water and turn left to join the narrow tarred road. This continues for 2km past Ardgartan campsite and youth hostel on the shore of Loch Long. You may see canoes in the water or hear a train on the far shore, rumbling along the West Highland Line, heading north to Fort William or Oban or south to Glasgow.

The road gradually rises, passing tall fir trees. At a large layby turn sharp right up a forestry road, where a sign announces Cat Craig Road. As this road steadily rises through stands of larch trees, views of Loch Long and The Brack gradually unfold.

The chaos of boulders and outcrops on The Brack's slopes becomes more striking. The mountain gets its name from the Gaelic *breac*, meaning mottled, just as Robert Louis Stevenson's real-life antihero in *Kidnapped* was called Alan Breck Stewart because of his pock-marked face.

Glen Croe is a U-shaped glacial valley which shed much of its debris into Loch Long at Ardgartan. Huge rocks perched on each side of the glen are the moraine left by the ice which receded only 10,000 years ago. A close study of roadside boulders may reveal beautiful, silvery undulating layers of mica-schist, a rock which was formed under intense heat and pressure.

There is a brief hiccup in the route as you reach the end of the forestry road and follow steps and a path uphill to a wooden footbridge built by young members of the Prince's Trust. The bridge was opened by the Prince of Wales in 1982.

Follow the track briefly downhill before joining another forestry road which swings round into the glen. The Cobbler emerges like a wall in front of you, but its unmistakable pronged summit cannot be seen from this angle.

The road continues uphill until it meets another forestry road leading back downhill to the visitor centre. If you wish to climb The Brack, continue for almost 1km until you pass a small rock wall, marked with drill grooves for explosives used to clear the way for the road. Soon you come to a green waymarker pointing left.

A white pole marks the start of the track. The first 100m or so leads through a plantation where the going can be muddy. Another 200m takes you to a fence with a stile and a sign warning that dogs should be on leads. Follow the track marked by white posts to the Bealach Dubh lic, the gap where the track descends to Lochgoilhead.

You are now in hill walking country. The traffic on the A83 is well out of hearing, and all around is bog and boulders.

The Brack's relatively benign western slope faces you. To climb it, follow the track until you are past the fifth post from the bealach, then head uphill. You will see a burn coming down the slope; keep to the right of this until it disappears, then trend right, up the grassy slope which gives a steady climb to the summit.

The effort will have been worth it as the view from the top is one of the best in the Southern Highlands. A roll call of the closest hills can be reeled off: Beinn an Lochain, Beinn Ime, The Cobbler. Further east is Ben Lomond, and there is a fine view south down Loch Long, with the tall tower of Inverkip power station rising from the Renfrewshire coastline on the Firth of Clyde.

Looking south from the summit of the Brack.

Retrace your steps carefully, remembering that descents can often be trickier underfoot than ascents. Back at the forestry road, turn right and follow the road to the junction then take the road leading downhill, back to the visitor centre.

The Brack from the head of Loch Long.

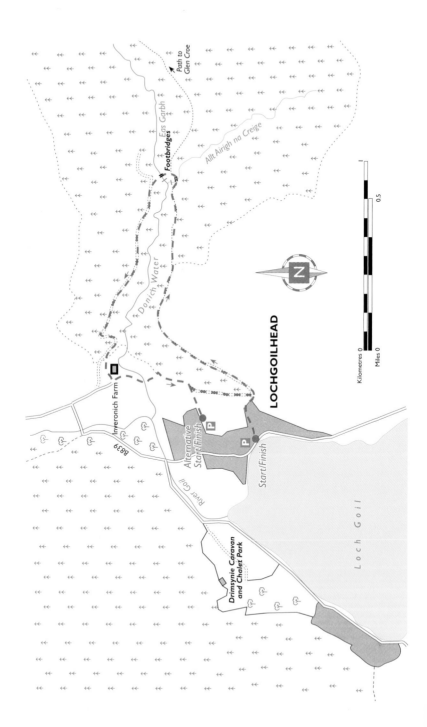

Path to
Glen Croe

Eas Garbh

Footbridges

Allt Airigh na Creige

Donich Water

**LOCHGOILHEAD**

Inveronich Farm

B839

Alternative
Start/Finish

P

P

Start/Finish

River Goil

Drimsynie Caravan
and Chalet Park

Loch Goil

Kilometres 0

Miles 0

0.5

N

# DONICH WATER

Few villages in the Highlands have a more attractive setting than Lochgoilhead. As its name states, it sits at the head of Loch Goil, a beautiful sea loch which is a branch of Loch Long. Because of its setting and its closeness to Glasgow, the village attracted the attention of Victorian businessmen who built villas along the shore. The loch, however, is not the only water attraction in the area. Behind the village is the lovely, wooded Glen Donich. Through the glen flows Donich Water, which joins the River Goil to flow into the loch.

The Donich Water route is short but fun: an ideal excursion for children who can enjoy picnicking in exciting surroundings and, with proper supervision, a clamber around rocks and pools.

From the shore car park, cross the main street and walk up the lane opposite, past the public toilets. The lane reaches the bottom of the hillside. Head right for a short distance until you see a forestry road heading uphill to the left. Up ahead is a green post with a red roundel, identifying the walk.

Walk up the forestry road, which has a plantation on its left. The grassy hillside to your right is covered in a

## INFORMATION

**Distance:** 4km (2.5miles).

**Start and finish:** Lochgoilhead shore car park.

**Terrain:** Forestry road and riverside paths. No special footwear needed.

**Public transport:** Weirs Tours bus from Helensburgh. Stagecoach Western Scottish from Dunoon.

**Refreshments:** Hotel at Lochgoilhead.

Exploring the banks of Donich Water.

mixture of gorse, holly, rhododendrons and silver birch trees. Further up the track, signs indicate a short cut back to Lochgoilhead and the forest walk ahead.

Continue uphill into the wood where you can hear Donich Water getting louder. At a part where you reach some steps, a track goes down to the burn. Here, it is possible to clamber onto large rocks and a small island in the middle of the burn, just the place for a break. Be very careful where you place your feet, however, because larch needles and exposed, smooth tree roots can be very slippery.

The track leads on to the first of two bridges which cross waterfalls that plunge into large rock pools. The first bridge crosses the Eas Garbh (*rough falls*), and the second, the Allt Airigh na Creige (*burn of the rocky shieling*). Both of these burns join up below the bridges to form Donich Water.

Vantage point over waterfall.

The source of the Eas Garbh is north-east in Coire Odhar, between the Brack (Walk 3) and Ben Donich. The line of hills stretching south down the Ardgoil peninsula from Lochgoilhead have acquired the name Argyll's Bowling Green. This is not a tongue-in-cheek reference to the rugged terrain, but an English play on the Gaelic *Buaile na Greine,* which means sunny cattle fold. This refers to a welcome piece of pasture where the Campbells would feed their cattle on the way to market.

After you cross the second bridge, the track enters a conifer plantation and heads downhill, back towards Lochgoilhead. The village was for almost 50 years the home of W. H. Murray, the renowned mountaineer and author who died in 1996 aged 83. Murray was among the leading climbers of the generation who established a renaissance in Scottish winter climbing in the 1930s. His book, *Mountaineering in Scotland,* is a classic of mountaineering literature, and his deeply-researched biography of Rob Roy Macgregor, and *The Companion Guide to the West Highlands of Scotland* are still avidly read.

Young canoeists return from an outing on Loch Goil.

Meanwhile, back at the walk, continue downhill through the forest. From here you can look west to the pointed peaks of Mullach Coire a' Chuir and Beinn Tharsuinn. When you have descended to Inveronich Farm, turn right and go past sheep dips. When you reach a road, turn left and go over a stile beside a galvanised steel gate.

Cross a bridge over Donich Water and continue along the track, or turn right along a narrower track beside Donich Water. A sign for the red mountain bike trail is at the entrance to the latter track. You soon reach the village. An alternative start and finish to the walk is from the Argyll Forest Park car park opposite the fire station.

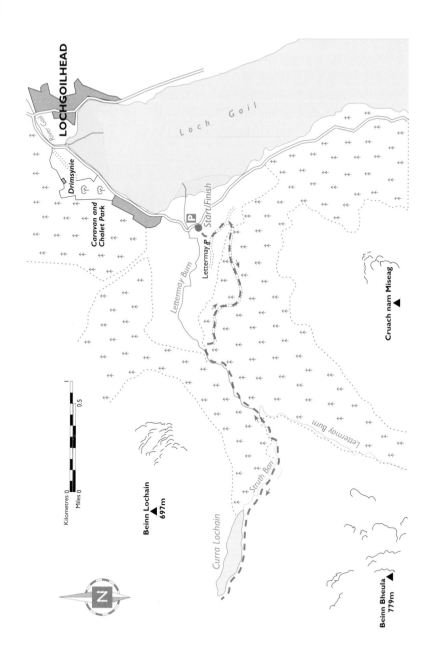

# CURRA LOCHAIN

I n the space of only three kilometres, this walk takes you through several environments, from a wooded lochside to a lochan on the edge of a bleak moor. On the way you pass through a forestry plantation and stand by the edge of a dramatic waterfall with views over Lochgoilhead and the mountains beyond.

## INFORMATION

**Distance:** 7km (4.5 miles).

**Start and finish:** Mouth of Lettermay Burn, Lochgoilhead. Take A83 to the Rest and Be Thankful and turn left onto B828 for Lochgoilhead.

**Terrain:** Good forest road and hill tracks, and some steep but easy scrambling. Walking shoes or boots recommended.

**Public transport:** Weirs Tours buses from Helensburgh, Stagecoach Western Scottish from Dunoon.

**Refreshments:** Hotel at Lochgoilhead.

Overlooking Lochgoilhead, from the forestry road.

The walk begins near the mouth of the Lettermay burn which flows into Loch Goil, opposite the village of Lochgoilhead. This area is only an hour's drive from Glasgow and has become increasingly popular with visitors, partly because of leisure developments which have taken place at Drimsynie Estate on the northwest shore of the loch.

Just as Argyll fell under the control of the Campbells, this corner of Cowal has become "Campbell's Kingdom". The Campbell in question is Douglas Campbell, a sheep farmer who went on to own the community's three hotels and establish an award-winning sheep and wool centre and large holiday chalet park. The scale of Mr Campbell's interests, and one incident in particular, involving the felling of oak trees on a site where he had intended to build houses, have caused controversy especially among local people. However Mr Campbell has been credited by the Scottish Tourist Board with bringing life and jobs to the area.

To find the start, head south, past the chalets, and cross the Lettermay burn. Cars can be parked in a pull-in area beside the track leading down to the old bridge. To start the walk, continue south for a few metres and turn right, up towards white-harled cottages.

Turn left onto a forestry road which, after about 200m, swings right and heads uphill to a forestry plantation. Cross a stile beside the gate at the plantation entrance and continue uphill. To the south, overlooking the road, you can see the tusky outcrops on the ridge leading up to the summit of Cruach nam Miseag.

When you reach a split in the road, take the right fork which leads down to a red brick pumphouse and weir at the Lettermay burn. Here, if you take care, you can explore a small, picturesque waterfall.

Continuing the walk, a white post marks the start of a track up the south bank of the burn. This is an idyllic stretch, with water rushing over flat rocks then slowing up through shallow pools. The walking here is easy, though boggy after rain, and you can enjoy the sight of

A flower blooms at the base of the Struth Ban waterfall.

mature conifers in the foreground and the slopes of Beinn Lochain on the horizon.

About 500m past the pumphouse you reach the point where the Lettermay burn meets Sruth Ban, the burn which forms the waterfall you are heading for. Use easy stepping stones to cross the Lettermay, which has swung in from the left.

Turn right and continue uphill by the south bank of Sruth Ban. Alternatively, turn left for a few yards and cut through a gap in a plantation which takes you to a fence with an opening and a stile. This takes you through a

On the south bank of
Lettermay Burn.

clearing in a young spruce plantation to the base of
the waterfall. The south bank of Sruth Ban is more
boggy but gives a more attractive approach to the fall.
Following the bank, you come to a fence which is
crossed easily, then 200m further on you turn a corner
to find the waterfall plunging down the hillside.

Continue climbing the south bank of Sruth Ban until
you rejoin the track which leads up past the fall. From
this height you can look down towards Lochgoilhead,
and beyond to the rugged backdrop of Ben Donich,
the Brack and the Cobbler.

As you continue up the track you will come to a rock
band running across the hillside. To find an easy way
through, head left to where the band peters out.
Rejoin the track as it heads up through grass and
bracken to meet the burn above the fall.

The track now follows the burn up onto a much
sterner landscape where the slope of Beinn Lochain,
up to the right, is a chaos of large boulders. When the
ground flattens out, you soon come to lonely Curra
Lochain, the marshy lochan, in the pass between
Beinn Lochain and Beinn Bheula.

Return by the same route, enjoying the views across
Loch Goil.

Road to Lochgoilhead

**CARRICK CASTLE**
*Start*

Carrick Castle
(remains)

*Loch Goil*

*Rubha Ardnahein*

Ardnahein Farm

*Loch Long*

*Knap*

Stronvochlan Farm

P

*Finart Bay*

**COULPORT**

*Finish* **ARDENTINNY**

A880

N

Kilometres 0 ──────── 1
Miles 0 ──────── 0.5

# CARRICK CASTLE TO ARDENTINNY

Anyone wishing to forget the ills of the world should not try this walk. The route may be one of the most beautiful in this book, but it contains jarring reminders of man's appetite for conflict and the brutality which was such a large element of Argyll's colourful history.

The walk begins at Carrick Castle, the village at the south-western end of Loch Goil. The castle itself is a three-storey tower house perched on a rock which juts into the loch. The castle belonged to the Campbells and was used by James IV for hunting wild boar. It

Carrick Castle.

acquired a sinister reputation when prisoners of the Campbells were held under grim conditions.

In 1685 the castle was burned as punishment for the Campbells' support of the Duke of Monmouth's unsuccessful rebellion against James VII. It has since been restored as a residence. It will be more pleasant, no doubt, than when it housed Patrick Lamont, a leading member of the clan which gradually lost control of Cowal to the Campbells. Patrick joined an attack on Campbell land in 1645. A year later, the Campbells retaliated in force and Patrick was imprisoned at Carrick Castle. Despite the Campbells' promise that Lamont lives would be spared, Patrick was taken to Inveraray and killed.

INFORMATION

**Distance:** 8km (5miles).

**Start:** Carrick Castle, Loch Goil.

**Finish:** Ardentinny, Loch Long.

**Terrain:** Mainly good forestry roads, with shorter stretches of shore walking and possibly boggy woodland paths. Light walking trainers or shoes generally adequate.

**Public transport:** Weirs Tours buses from Helensburgh, and Stagecoach Western Scottish buses from Dunoon, to Carrick Castle. Stagecoach from Dunoon to Ardentinny.

**Refreshments:** hotels at Carrick Castle and Ardentinny.

Head south from the village along the shore road. Where the tarmac ends and the road becomes gravel, look back at the castle and the impressive view up to Lochgoilhead. Continue along the gravel road towards Ardnahein farm. To the right of the farm's private entrance sign is an Ardentinny sign with a green roundel, the marker for this route.

Follow the track alongside a farm building and past the edge of the farm, then climb steps over a fence. Cross a field where sheep are often grazing to a rocky causeway beside the shore, taking care on the slippery rocks. Head for a shingle point, to avoid boggy ground. Go round the point and follow the shore, with attractive pebbles, back towards trees where a marker post indicates a boulder that can be stepped on to climb over a fence.

Follow the track uphill, away from the shore, and cross a stile over another fence. Cross a footbridge over a burn to get into the wood. Here the track is more

defined, but muddy in parts. One of the walk's highlights is climbing up through this birchwood, getting glimpses through the trees of the loch and the hills on the opposite shore.

You soon enter a firebreak through a dense

Looking north from the birchwood to the head of Loch Goil.

Sitka spruce plantation. About 70m along, a tree blocks the way. Turn this on the right, then continue along the break for some distance, crossing streams by duckboards.

The break eventually joins a forestry road near a tall electricity pylon. Turn left down the road, which cuts through a rocky gap with a tall cliff on the left. The road drops down to Loch Long, where you can see not only the water sparkling through the trees but also first signs of major excavation on the opposite bank.

You have to pass the old cottage at Knap, where tree harvesting has taken place, to see what has developed on the eastern shore. The high tower of Inverkip power station in Renfrewshire may dominate the skyline to the south, but it is the large steel building opposite which grabs attention. This is the explosives handling jetty at Coulport, built to load nuclear warheads on and off the Royal Navy's Trident submarines.

A few miles further east in the Gare Loch is the Trident base itself at Faslane with its massive shiplift, designed to raise 16,000-tonne nuclear submarines out of the water for repair. The Coulport jetty lies directly opposite Ardentinny, and as you approach it you may see small inflatable boats zipping around the loch on security patrol.

The forest road gradually rises high above the loch to give your first sight of Ardentinny, nestling to the south of Finart Bay. Where the road meets a junction, take the left fork downhill to a broadleaf wood. The road continues down past Stronvochlan farm to the bay, where there is a car park and picnic benches. A short walk along the shore takes you to Ardentinny itself.

The name for this pretty village with its old hotel means *headland of the fire*, possibly referring to a signal fire once lit to summon the old ferry that ran over to Coulport.

Near the end of the walk: Stronvochlan Farm, Ardentinny.

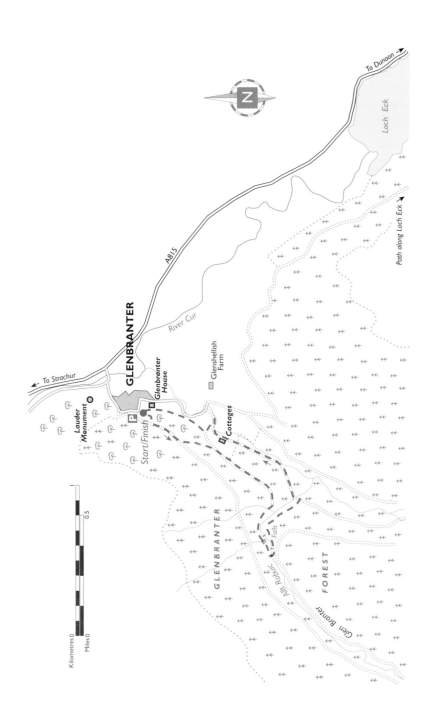

# GLENBRANTER

At the head of Loch Eck, a beautiful ribbon of fresh water stretching about six miles down the centre of the Cowal Peninsula, lies Glenbranter. It takes its name from the estate owned by Sir Harry Lauder, the Scottish music hall artist, in his day one of the most popular entertainers in the world. The estate was a peaceful retreat from performing at home and abroad, but became a place of sadness for Sir Harry and Lady Lauder when they heard there on New Year's Day 1917 that their son, John, had been killed in action in France. John had been a Captain in the Argyll and Sutherland Highlanders. The Lauders could not bear to remain at Glenbranter, so they moved to the Dunoon area.

In 1921 the Forestry Commission acquired Glenbranter Forest and started planting spruce, as part of the drive to replenish timber stocks devoured by the First World War. Soon after, the commission offered the Royal Botanic Garden in Edinburgh land at Glenbranter for planting rhododendrons and other plants from the Himalaya. Although the Royal Botanic Garden soon moved to Benmore, at the south end of Loch Eck, many different varieties of rhododendron from that original planting may be found on this walk.

In 1935, Glenbranter Forest became part of the new Argyll Forest Park, set up by the Commission with the co-operation of Glasgow Corporation, which was a major landowner. This was Scotland's first forest park, where the public had access for recreation. The park covers almost 25,000 hectares of mountain, moorland and woods west of Loch Long.

In the 1950s, a village of timber houses was built by the Forestry Commission for its workers at Glenbranter. Long before, the area was noted for its hardwoods,

## INFORMATION

**Distance:** 3.25km (2miles).

**Start and finish:** Lauder Walks car park, Glenbranter, 4km south of Strachur on A815 road.

**Terrain:** Good forest paths with few steep stretches. No special footwear needed.

**Public transport:** Stagecoach Western Scottish Dunoon-Inveraray buses pass village on A815.

**Refreshments:** Hotels at Strachur and on Loch Eck-side.

The forest village of Glenbranter.

which were turned into charcoal used for iron smelting at Furnace, south of Inveraray.

Close to the village is a network of walks, the Lauder Forest Walks, which begin at a car park near the site of Sir Harry's home, Glenbranter House. The longest and most interesting walk leads to waterfalls on the Allt Robuic burn, which flows down the glen. This route, still relatively short, is identified along the way by yellow marker posts.

From the end of the car park, take a path where a sign says Lauder Walks. Pass a green waymarker post with blue, yellow and red notches. The deciduous trees and conifers here were originally planted as an attractive setting for Glenbranter House. Take a right fork uphill to a forestry road. Leave the road after about 100m and cut downhill to the left on a path.

Waterfall in Lauder forest.

The path reaches another forestry road with a sign pointing left to the car park and right to the Lauder Walks, with a bench at a viewpoint overlooking the village. Turn right, uphill, and follow a forestry road through a plantation, still young enough to allow a view down the glen. The route now goes through an area of large, mature conifers before you reach the end of the forestry road. Walk down steps and turn right at the Lauder Walk signs.

A path clings to the side of a gorge, and further up leads to a viewpoint at a small waterfall. After heavy rainfall you can hear the burn rushing below. The path is well gravelled, giving good grip, and is protected by wooden railings. However, care must always be taken of young children.

Soon you cross a wooden footbridge over a waterfall. Enjoyable though this is, it is just a minor prelude to what appears round the corner - a bigger waterfall which, in spate, surges down the cliff at the head of the glen. Another footbridge takes you over the Allt Robuic burn and then back downhill by its right bank. As you descend you can see on the other side of the burn the first waterfall you passed, an elegant veil compared to the bigger fall higher up.

The path reaches a forestry road where you turn left and walk past cottages. About 200m after the cottages turn left, back towards the wood. Waymarkers show where you turn right and follow the edge of the wood by a path which leads you back to the car park.

A trip to Glenbranter should be completed by visiting John Lauder's memorial, a short distance from the car park. The memorial is in a small graveyard overlooking the A815 Strachur-Dunoon road. To reach it, leave the car park, walk past the village and turn right onto the main road. Walk south for about 300m and climb a signposted path to the cemetery on the north side of the road. From here you can see Glenbranter estate, the village, and the hills overlooking Loch Eck.

John Lauder's memorial.

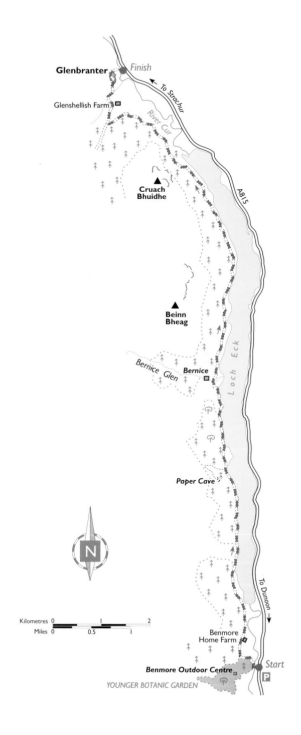

# LOCH ECK

Lock Eck slashes its way down the Cowal Peninsula like a swordstroke through bracken. This thin sliver of water set in wooded, mountainous surroundings is one of the most beautiful parts of Argyll. This walk follows a good forestry road along the west shore of Loch Eck. The only difficulty is provided by a brief, optional clamber up a hillside to a historic cave.

The walk begins at the south end of the loch, at the Younger Botanic Garden at Benmore. This estate was gifted to the nation in 1925 by a member of the famous Younger family of Edinburgh, associated with the making of fine beers and Younger's Tartan. Four years later the garden became an outpost of the Royal Botanic Garden in Edinburgh.

## INFORMATION

**Distance:** Distance: 13km (8 miles).

**Start:** Younger Botanic Garden, Benmore.

**Finish:** Glenbranter village.

**Terrain:** Mostly good forestry road. Route to 'Paper Cave' involves very steep climb over smooth rock. Shoes with cleated, rubber soles recommended.

**Public transport:** Stagecoach Western Scottish buses pass Benmore Gardens and Glenbranter road end.

**Refreshments:** Cafe at Benmore Gardens.

Dusk on Loch Eck.

The garden, which is run as a scientific establishment, attracts thousands of visitors a year. An avenue of giant redwood and 250 varieties of rhododendron form only part of the collection at Benmore, and a vital part of the work done there is the cultivation of plants which are endangered in their homelands. An example of this are the Japanese umbrella pines, which form the largest group of their kind anywhere in the world.

The Loch Eck walk starts at the entrance to Benmore, off the A815 Strachur-Dunoon road. Walk past the cafe and shop and turn right after the bridge over the River Eachaig. The road you are following soon swings left and heads uphill towards the old mansionhouse steading.

Beyond the clocktower is a sign pointing right for Bernice and Benmore Home Farm. Here, the road heads north towards the loch, passing a large boulder festooned with bolts for rock climbing practice.

You soon reach the southern end of Loch Eck, and can see points of land coming down to both shorelines in layer upon layer, leading off into the distance. The tarmac road ends beside a sewage treatment works, and you cross a stile to join the gravel road which continues the rest of the way up the lochside. Loch Eck and Loch Lomond are the only places where the powan, a freshwater relative of the herring can be found. The fish were trapped after the lochs became cut off from the sea during the last Ice Age, about 10,000 years ago.

As you continue, the sound of traffic drifts across from the main road which skirts the east shore. Further north, opposite the Coylet Hotel, you pass a rock overhang. Soon after you turn a long, lefthand corner until you can see pasture jutting into the loch. On the left is a small parking area for cars; it is here that a track leads into the woods and uphill to the Paper Cave.

This cave is said to have been the place where the Campbells kept their deeds and other important documents safe when their lands were being raided by their enemy, the Duke of Atholl. This followed the failed 1685 uprising by the ninth Duke of Argyll against the Catholic King James VI. The ninth duke, who was executed, was an exception to the line of astute Campbell chieftains who knew that real power was won by politicking in Edinburgh, the capital, rather than fighting in the Highlands.

The approach to the cave is impeded in places by fallen trees. As you follow the track uphill, you get a breathtaking view of Loch Eck, looking north to Glenbranter. The upper part of the track demands extra care as it goes over steep and slippery rocks, where roots make useful handholds. You go past what you may think is the Paper Cave, some clefts in the rock, and continue up part of the hillside which turns out to be a huge flake. Behind this flake is a deep, wet and foreboding fissure, hardly a comforting place to hide from your enemies. The return from the Paper Cave must be treated with even greater care, as descents can be more awkward than climbs on steep ground.

The next landmark you pass is Bernice Glen. Bernice is from *bearnais*, the Gaelic for a gap, and this glen formed part of a route used by the Campbells to cross Argyll safely and quickly. The handsome, whitewashed house above the track is used as an outdoor centre by Edinburgh City Council.

Beyond Bernice, the road rises into mature conifer plantations. Above the trees, a line of rugged hills stretches from Beinn Bheag to Cruach Bhuidhe at the head of the loch. The road rises and falls, sometimes giving a good view of the loch, sometimes closed in by trees.

*Top:* Looking north up the loch from near the start of the walk.

*Bottom:* Looking south down Loch Eck from the west shore.

Eventually you are alongside the head of the loch. Here, opposite the whitewashed cottage on the opposite shore, the road splits. Take the uphill, left-hand fork, which soon starts to twist downhill through more woods for about 2km. The road then swings sharp right towards Glenshellish Farm and joins the bridge over the Glenshellish Burn, beside the farm.

Once over the burn, you reach the cottages referred to near the end of Walk 7, and continue to Glenbranter village.

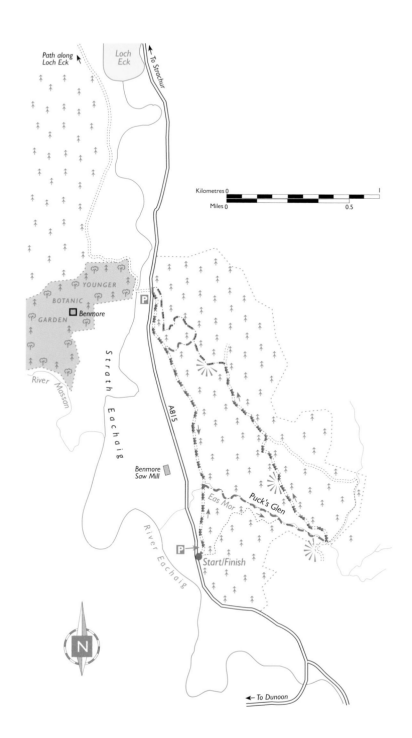

Path along
Loch Eck

Loch
Eck

To Strachur

Kilometres 0                                    1
Miles 0                              0.5

YOUNGER
BOTANIC
GARDEN

Benmore

River Massan

Strath Eachaig

A815

Benmore
Saw Mill

Eas Mor

Puck's Glen

River Eachaig

Start/Finish

N

To Dunoon

# PUCK'S GLEN

One of the best loved walks in Argyll is also one of its shortest. It is not brevity appealing to the lazy that makes Puck's Glen so popular, but the romantic, fairy grotto atmosphere of the gorge walk through the glen.

The gorge, though steep in places, should appeal so much to young children that they should be quite happy to make the ascent unaided. The walk was created in the last century by the Youngers brewing

## INFORMATION

**Distance:** 3km (1.87 miles).

**Start and finish:** Forestry Commission car park on east side of A815 Strachur-Dunoon Road, 1.5km south of Younger Botanic Garden.

**Terrain:** Good paths and forestry roads. No special footwear needed, but watch steep drops beside the route.

**Refreshments:** Tea room at Younger Botanic Garden. Good facilities in Dunoon.

**Public Transport:** Train and ferry from Glasgow to Dunoon. Stagecoach Western Scottish bus services between Dunoon-Strachur stop at Benmore Gardens.

**Opening hours:** Benmore: April-October, 10.00-18.00. Admission charge.

Entrance to Puck's Glen.

family of Edinburgh but fell into disrepair. The path was restored in 1986 with new bridges, steps and drainage ditches put in by workers as part of the former Manpower Service's community programme, in co-operation with the Forestry Commission.

The walk begins at the Forestry Commission car park on the east side of the A815, about 1.5km south of the entrance to the Younger Botanic Garden. From the car park, walk along the tarmac road parallel to the A815 until you reach the old metal milestone which reads 'Dunoon Pier 6 miles'.

Go through the kissing gate and join the path that follows the Eas Mor (*big fall*) burn uphill, past a

Waterfall in the glen.

fascinating succession of cascades and pools. Overhead, mosses cling to the rock walls of the gorge as water dribbles down. After about 500m you reach a point where a second path descends to the car park. At this junction, be careful of the steep 30m drop to the burn. Continue to the upper glen, where tall fir trees rise up from the tops of the rock walls.

Wet, misty weather does not spoil the walk, but, if anything, enhances the lush, mysterious and secluded nature of the glen. On bright days, a different side of the glen is revealed as the sun filters through the trees to cast light on shadowy corners.

Soon you reach a forestry road which runs across the hillside. Turn right to a viewpoint which shows a pleasant panorama of woods and hills towards Glen Massan, at the south end of Loch Eck. An extension to the walk uphill from Puck's Glen is closed off (summer 1996) because of fallen trees and erosion.

Continue north along the forestry road which takes you to the Black Gates, which form the entrance to the Younger Botanic Garden. Anyone with even the slightest interest in plants and trees should visit the garden, which is an outstation of the Royal Botanic Garden in Edinburgh. The garden benefits from the mild and wet Argyll climate and has over 200 kinds of conifer, some of which are rare varieties and are being grown to preserve their genetic strains.

About 300m from where the Puck's Glen path meets the forestry road you reach the best viewpoint, below which is a little picnic area made out of stone slabs. Continue along the forestry road until you reach a track leading downhill, marked by a sign saying Black Gates. You soon reach a third viewpoint. Continue down the track until you regain the tarmac road that you left to climb Puck's Glen.

Rhododendrons on the road back to the forest car park.

When you head back to the car park, keep a look out for beautiful trees on your left, particularly extremely tall Wellingtonia, known as punch trees because of their soft bark.

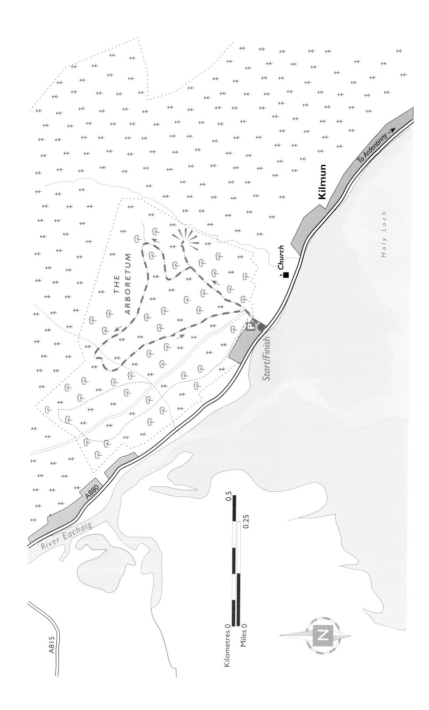

# KILMUN ARBORETUM

One of the central characters in Robin Jenkins' novel *The Cone Gatherers* is Calum, a simple hunchback who cannot walk through the woods of an Argyll estate without tripping and stumbling. High in a treetop, however, Calum moves with sureness and grace as he picks cones for the war effort, whereas Duror, the embittered gamekeeper who plots his downfall, finds himself sick with fear when he tries to clamber more than a few feet off the ground.

Anyone who has read *The Cone Gatherers* will catch the atmosphere of the book's fictional forest when they visit Kilmun Arboretum. The arboretum, which is not far, incidentally, from the home of Robin Jenkins, can be seen for many miles. It is sited on the steep western slope of the Strone Peninsula at the head of the Holy Loch. This 'forest garden' or collection of experimental plots planted with a wide variety of trees was established in the 1930s by the Forestry Commission.

Kilmun has long been a popular place to visit. It was named after St Mun, an Irish disciple of St Columba, who is said to have established a chapel here, making the area one of the leading centres of Christianity in Argyll. This is believed to be the reason why the Holy Loch got its name; the prefix *kil*, which is frequently found in Argyll (Kilmichael, Kilchattan etc), is the Gaelic word for chapel or cell. According to Lord Cockburn, the famous judge who wrote about his circuit journeys around Scotland, Kilmun 150 years ago was "a delightful retreat from the mill, the bank and the bench".

The entrance to the arboretum is about 100m north of Kilmun Parish Church, which has the mausoleum of the powerful Campbells of Argyll in its graveyard. There is a car park about 200m from the main road. There are three walks marked out by coloured posts, and they range in length from half a kilometre to just

## INFORMATION

**Distance:** 2.25km (1.5 miles).

**Start and Finish:** Kilmun, Holy Loch.

**Terrain:** Mostly good paths, but stout footwear needed on very muddy and steep stretches. Care needed where polished tree roots exposed.

**Public transport:** Stagecoach Western Scottish bus services to Dunoon.

**Refreshments:** Local hotels.

At the top of the walk, looking across the Holy Loch to Sandbank.

over 2km. The longest one, described here, is called the Alpine Walk, and it rises to give excellent views of the Holy Loch and down to Sandbank and Dunoon.

From the car park, take the path that starts beside the information board and slants uphill to the right. Here you pass North American hemlock and maple, the first of a wide variety of exotic trees you will see along the way.

Each tree is identified by posts giving its name in English and Latin. Just before a low wall you find an example of the tallest tree in the world, the Pacific Coast Redwood or *Sequoia Sempenvirens*. In their native region, the Pacific Coast of North America, they grow to 110m in height but in Europe they grow to about 40m.

A carpet of bluebells.

Further up the slope, take a right branch in the path to head uphill for about 40m to a viewpoint. Here you can see ferries crossing the Firth of Clyde, a reminder of how quickly people can travel from the centre of Glasgow to Cowal or Bute. Return to the main path which starts to rise steeply. Be careful if the ground is muddy as the slope falls away abruptly from the path. Continue uphill past a stand of Rocky Mountain fir, which have short branches.

Go onto the upper section of the walk, parts of which can be extremely muddy, with exposed tree roots which are slippery. Cross an open grassy area then head downhill through one of the many areas where bluebells bloom in abundance in the spring and early summer.

A footbridge crosses a burn, and soon afterwards the path reaches a sharp, left-hand corner before the descent. Take care as you go round the corner because exposed tree roots can be treacherous and there is a steep slope below the path.

At this point you can see the head of Holy Loch directly below, and south to Sandbank and Dunan, the hill that is climbed in the Ardnadam Glen walk. Walk down the path until you reach a blue 'Alpine Walk' waymarker post beside a group of silver birch trees, just before a bridge. Leave the Alpine Walk here to turn right and follow another path slightly uphill to join the 'Eucalyptus Walk', which has red posts.

Fungus on a silver birch.

From the first red post, the path heads downhill past a wide variety of fir trees. Shortly before you join a forestry road, Antarctic beech with their tiny leaves present a charming picture. The highlight of this second walk is the Eucalyptus trees themselves, instantly recognisable by their peeling reddish bark and smoky blue/green leaves. These tall trees greet you as you step onto the forestry road and turn left to walk down the final stretch to the car park.

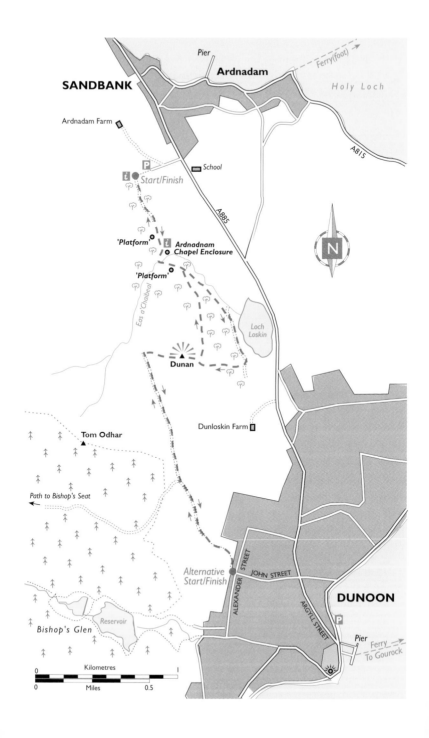

Pier

**Ardnadam**

**SANDBANK**

Ferry (foot)

*Holy Loch*

Ardnadam Farm

A815

*P*

*i* ● *Start/Finish*

School

A885

'Platform'

*i*

○ **Ardnadnam Chapel Enclosure**

'Platform'

*Eas o'Chaibeal*

*Loch Loskin*

**Dunan**

Dunloskin Farm

**Tom Odhar**

*Path to Bishop's Seat*

*Alternative Start/Finish*

ALEXANDER STREET

JOHN STREET

**DUNOON**

ARGYLL STREET

*P*

Pier

Ferry To Gourock

*Reservoir*

*Bishop's Glen*

| 0 | | Kilometres | | 1 |
| 0 | Miles | | 0.5 | |

# ARDNADAM GLEN

O n the map it's called Dunan, but to locals the low, rounded hill which forms the highest point of this walk is the Camel's Hump. Though only 198m high, this hill, behind Dunoon and Sandbank, is justly popular among local walkers for its outstanding view not only over the surrounding countryside but also of the Firth of Clyde and the Holy Loch.

## INFORMATION

**Distance:** 7km (4.3 miles).

**Start and finish:** Top of John Street, Dunoon.

**Terrain:** Mainly well surfaced paths, with short stretches of rougher ground which may be boggy. No special footwear needed.

**Public Transport:** Trains from Glasgow Central Station to Gourock for CalMac ferries to Dunoon. Buses from Buchanan Bus Station, Glasgow, to McInroy's Point for Western ferries to Hunter's Quay. Wide variety of Cowal buses to and from Dunoon and Sandbank.

**Refreshments:** Wide choice, particularly in Dunoon.

Looking across the Holy Loch to Kilmun from the summit of Dunan.

It is not surprising, therefore, that Dunan (locally pronounced Doonan) might have been a vantage point in prehistoric times. A ring of boulders near the summit strongly suggests it was the site of the *little fort* which Dunan means in Gaelic. Prehistory is the main theme of this walk, and a small, nondescript hollow below Dunan, rather than the Camel's Hump itself, is the focus of attention. This hollow is Ardnadam Glen, where archaeological digs in an enclosure have revealed a wealth of remains dating from 3,000BC.

There are two starts to this walk. From the village of Sandbank, long famous for yacht building (two Americas Cup challengers were constructed there), you can follow the A885 road towards Dunoon and turn right near the Sandbank boundary sign. A narrow road leads to a car park and an information board with leaflets in a box at the entrance to the Ardnadam heritage trail.

Entrance to the walk.

The alternative way to the trail may be more convenient for visitors. This shares the first section of Walk 13 (Bishop's Glen), starting at the top of John Street in Dunoon. To follow this route cross over Alexander Street, join a forest road and continue for 500m until you reach a second forestry road, branching right.

This second road continues gradually uphill behind Dunan for almost 1km. At the road end, a track heads east through a tussocky forestry break to the summit of Dunan, where a viewfinder identifies landmarks. From the summit, a well-worn track drops briefly east before swinging north to Ardnadam Glen. On the descent you pass numbered posts which aid interpretation, in conjunction with the information leaflets produced by Argyll & Bute Countryside Trust.

Beyond post 9, follow electricity pylons through a forestry break. The track then drops steeply down through boggy ground before passing a fork where a more defined path cuts back south-east through the lower part of the woods to Loch Loskin. You will take this path later in the walk.

Continuing roughly north, you will see on the right some flat ground among trees. This is a recessed platform, believed to have been the site of a timber roundhouse. After a burn, the path becomes much smoother.

Soon you arrive at the enclosure where information boards and posts of differing shapes and colours help create a picture of how different communities existed here. The site of the first settlement, a neolithic house from 3,000 BC, is marked out, as is the site of an iron age roundhouse from about 2,000 years ago. Still visible are the foundations of a chapel built 1,000 years ago, said to be the most recent building in the glen. A detailed description of what was discovered in the enclosure can be found in the book *Ardnadam Glen* by Elizabeth B Rennie, a leading member of the Cowal Archaeological and Historical Society, which carried out the digs.

Please Do Not Walk On The Chapel Walls They Are 1000 Years Old

Remains of chapel.

The well-surfaced path continues north, passing another recessed platform beside post 3 and going underneath a hazel tree forming a natural arch. It is worth continuing the short distance to the start of the heritage trail in the hope of picking up the excellent leaflet from the box at the information board.

From the trail entrance, retrace your steps along the path and past the enclosure to the fork, where the right-hand branch led you down from Dunan. Take the left branch, a recently improved path leading through a beautiful oakwood. Gravel and duckboards, though unsightly, ease the way over boggy ground. After a few hundred metres you cross a small bridge over a ditch. Join a track which follows a fence bordering the field in which you will see Loch Loskin. It is a pity that power lines spoil the view of this small, attractive loch rich in wildfowl.

At the end of the fence, a gate controls private access to Dunloskin Farm. On the right, however, another small bridge crosses the ditch, taking you back into the wood. Follow a track uphill through the trees. At a fork, take the right branch uphill to a wide avenue through the trees created by recent felling. The path then runs briefly up the edge of a plantation to join, beside post 10, the track you took from the Dunan summit.

Return to the summit and retrace your steps to Dunoon.

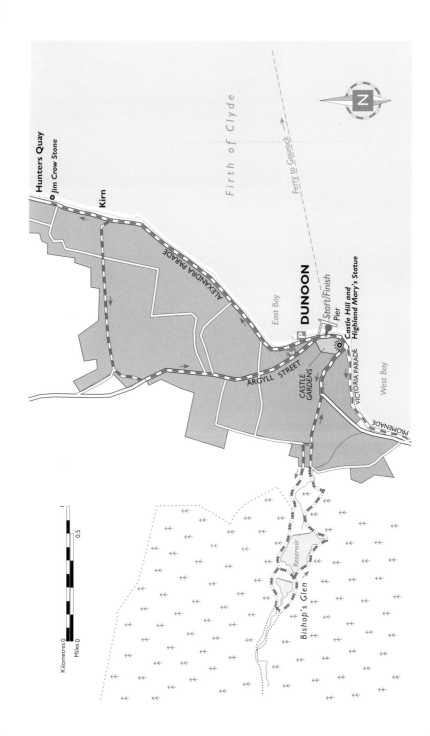

# DUNOON TOWN WALK

Tired? Stressed out? Needing to spend a quiet weekend in a peaceful seaside town? Then you'd better stay clear of Dunoon on the last Saturday of August. If you go down to Argyll Street, the town's main street, in the evening of that day, you will be joined in your promenade by happy revellers and more than 100 pipe bands. The annual 'March of 1,000 Pipers' draws visitors from all over Scotland and abroad. This spectacular event marks the end of the Cowal Highland Gathering, said to be the world's biggest Highland Games.

Eavesdrop on kilted youngsters in the street or in Dunoon Stadium, where the Games are held, and you are as likely to hear a Canadian or Australian accent as one from Argyll. Check the programme, and the list of competitors includes dancers and pipers from Michigan, Ontario, Johannesburg, Tasmania and countless other places which became the destination for Highlanders forced out of their glens by poverty and clearance.

There is a buzz about Dunoon that is not restricted to the Gathering. The town is the hub of Cowal, and its closest contact point to Glasgow, only 95 minutes away by ferry and train. Dunoon is remarkable for its ability to absorb large numbers of new people without losing its character. The influx of personnel from the US Navy submarine base on Holy Loch testified to this. Annual invasions of summer tourists arriving by steamer was an earlier example of this talent to accommodate strangers.

The Americans left in 1992, and trips 'doon the watter' are not as popular as they once were, but the area is now seeking a bigger share of the growing 'green tourism' market which includes all those people interested in walking.

The best way to approach Dunoon is by sea, and the first impression is of the pretty, cream and chocolate-

## INFORMATION

**Distance:** 7km (4.3 miles)

**Start and finish:** Dunoon Pier.

**Terrain:** Pavements, good paths in Bishop's Glen.

**Public Transport:** Bus services from throughout Cowal. Train from Glasgow Central Station to CalMac Ferry at Gourock.

**Refreshments:** Wide choice.

*Next page:* Jim Crow, with Western Ferries vessel and yachts in the background.

CalMac ferry arriving at
Dunoon Pier.

coloured Victorian pier building. How many people
landed here from Glasgow, excited about a holiday
away from the crush and smoke of the city?
Interestingly, the Firth of Clyde had a previous
connection with American military affairs: the river's
fast steamers were bought up by the Confederates
during the Civil War to run the blockade established
by the North. As a result, more modern passenger
steamers had to be built to replace them.

Overlooking the pier is Castle Hill, which is thought
to have originally been the site of an iron age fort.
Little remains of the subsequent castle which became
the property of the heir to the Scottish throne. The
Castle Buildings nearby were the summer residence of
a Glasgow Lord Provost and are to become a museum.

On a small outcrop of Castle Hill stands the bronze
statue of Highland Mary: Mary Campbell, who was
one of the poet Robert Burns' lovers. Mary was born in
Dunoon and met Burns when she worked in service in
Ayrshire. The couple exchanged Bibles in an old
marriage rite, but Mary died soon after of a fever. Her
statue depicts her looking across the Firth of Clyde to
Burns' native Ayrshire.

Before leaving Castle Gardens, look for the Scottish
Film Council plaque commemorating Eric Campbell,

the Dunoon-born film actor who played the big, bearded bounder in countless Charlie Chaplin films. Other famous people belonging to or educated in Dunoon include another actor, Sylvester McCoy, who played Dr Who, and John Smith, the former Labour Party leader.

From the gardens, head up Tom-a Mhoid Road, the place where justice was meted out. Here, you will pass a memorial to the Lamonts who were sentenced to death by the Campbells in 1646. Follow signs which take you to Bishop's Glen via Auchamore Road, Alexander Street and Nelson Street. The glen is a popular beauty spot for townsfolk. A network of paths lead through woodland past Dunoon's old reservoirs, where fly fishing is popular. There is no chance of getting lost, as any path downhill takes you back into the town.

Back at the sea front, a pleasant walk can be enjoyed on Victoria Parade and the Promenade, south of the pier. There is plenty to see in the Firth of Clyde, a yachting paradise. Just offshore is the Gantocks, a partially sunken rock which has proved treacherous to sailors. A flashing beacon now gives warning to anyone who comes near. On the opposite shore, the tall chimney of Inverkip power station is a prominent landmark.

Heading north from the pier, you find the Dunoon area's quirkiest landmark. Jim Crow is the name given to the large boulder which sits on the shore between Kirn and Hunter's Quay. Painted to resemble a crow, this boulder is a huge lump of schist which was deposited possibly 20,000 years ago by a passing glacier.

A dance band plays for visitors beside the esplanade.

Back beside the pier, you can sit in front of the open air bandstand and tap your feet to local musicians playing country dance music. The bandstand area is quite new, and reflects the aim of the Cowal Initiative, a strategy set up to see Dunoon and Cowal into a new era of prosperity following the departure of the US Navy.

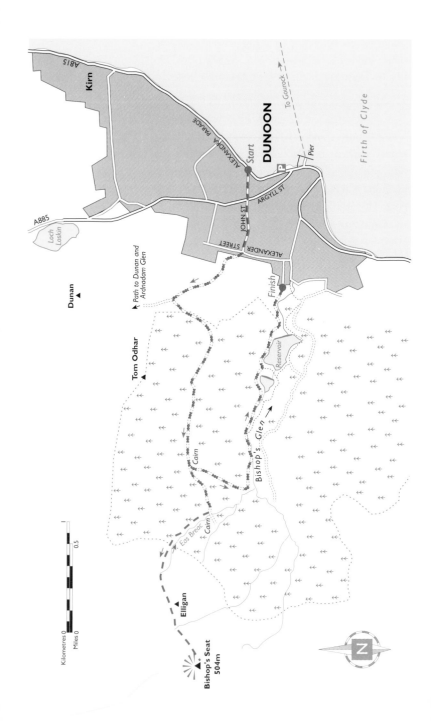

# BISHOP'S SEAT

Bishop's Seat is the sprawling, rounded hill which provides a tree-covered backdrop to Dunoon. The hill is said to have got its name from a Bishop of Dunoon who would take his exercise there every morning. Had His Grace made it to the summit every day, he would have been completing the equivalent of two Ben Nevis climbs a week.

Bishop's Glen is a walk that every self-respecting native of Dunoon has done at least once, and many

The rounded summit of Bishop's Seat, seen from the Coffin Road to the northwest.

enjoy it on a regular basis. Although the hill does not look dramatic, it is by no means a pushover. The walk to the 504m summit requires a reasonable amount of effort, and water-resistant footwear, and the reward is a wonderful and varied panorama.

The walk begins in John Street, which runs uphill from the seafront at Alexandra Parade, crossing Argyll Street, in the centre of town. At the top of John Street, cross Alexander Street and join a gravel forest road which turns briefly right before heading uphill and through a gate into a plantation.

As you go uphill, you pass the road to the right which goes towards Dunan. Soon, a good view can be had of Dunoon. Go past an old quarry beside a burn which flows through a break in the trees from the hill of Tom Odhar. When the road swings more to the left,

## INFORMATION

**Distance:** 8km (5 miles).

**Start:** Top of John Street, Dunoon.

**Finish:** Bishop's Glen, Dunoon.

**Terrain:** Good forestry road in plantation. Very wet ground in gap between Eilligan and Bishop's Seat. Muddy on parts of track leading to Bishop's Glen. Lightweight walking boots or trainers will do if you don't mind wet feet, otherwise wellingtons or stronger boots.

**Public transport:** Bus services throughout Cowal Peninsula to Dunoon. From Glasgow, train to Caledonian MacBrayne ferry terminal at Gourock. Half-hourly ferries to Dunoon.

**Refreshments:** Wide variety of cafes, restaurants and pubs in Dunoon.

you come past a second, larger quarry, and another burn flowing through a break. About 300m beyond the quarry is a cairn on the left which marks the track down to Bishop's Glen (Walk 12).

Continue up the road for a further 300m, passing a third quarry on the right, then walk a few hundred metres further until you reach a second cairn. This cairn, on the right-hand side where the road dips briefly and crosses a burn, marks the start of a path leading up to the upper slopes of Bishop's Seat.

Climb up a firebreak through the trees by following the right-hand side of the burn. The start of this stretch is through bracken, skirting trees to your right. Quite soon you leave the bracken for grass and heather where the path becomes more obvious.

The break continues uphill and reaches a left-hand corner where you can see the ridge which leads up to Eilligan, the hill which is Bishop's Seat's nearest neighbour. At the corner you can also see up the Firth of Clyde to Dumbarton Rock and the high flats of Glasgow, glinting in the sun.

Three drainage ditches must be crossed before you reach the top of the firebreak. Here, a fence heads south-west, away from the plantation and up onto the open hillside of Eilligan. This fence bypasses the summit of Eilligan and eventually takes you down to boggy low ground, then up to the summit of Bishop's Seat. A stream runs down from this gap between the two hills, so wet feet are almost guaranteed. Also, watch out for old fence-wire hidden in the ground like snares.

The summit of Bishop's Seat is soon reached from the gap. From the top a huge expanse of the Firth of Clyde can be seen, including the Cumbraes off Ayrshire, as well as a glimpse of Loch Eck, overlooked by the hills to the north-east.

Return to Eilligan where you will see, just below the summit, a large wooden cross mounted on a cairn. From this position you can look down the hillside, and

A good view of Dunoon
from the wooden cross
near the summit of
Eilligan.

over the trees to Dunoon's main reservoir in Bishop's
Glen. Further beyond is the town itself, with ferries
arriving at and leaving the pier.

From Eilligan, retrace your steps to the firebreak you
climbed to get on to the hillside. It is worth
remembering that as you follow the fence past the top
of the plantation, the break in question is the first one
you encounter after you reach the trees.

After you have walked down the break to the forestry
road, turn left and continue downhill until you reach
the cairn marking the track to Bishop's Glen. Turn
right here. The track, which is obvious though muddy
at times, leads down to the reservoirs. Here, there is a
wide variety of paths and tracks, including one which
passes over a small gorge, but there is no chance of
getting lost because all the routes downhill eventually
lead back to the town.

Looking down to the
Firth of Clyde from
forestry road.

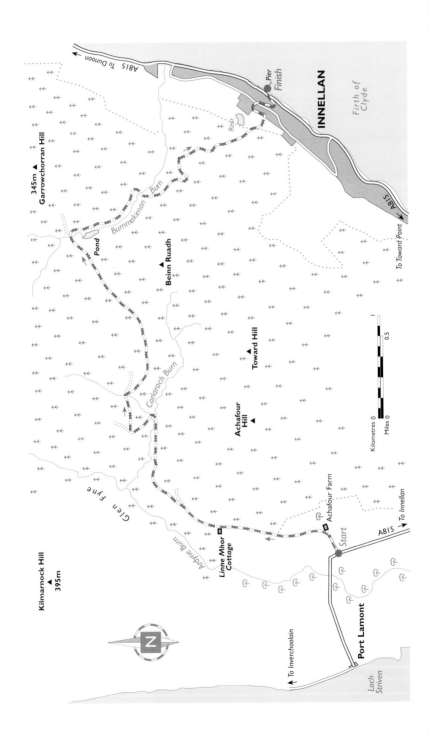

# ACHAFOUR-INNELLAN

To reach the start of this walk, you must pass a ruined tower, half-hidden among trees. Scotland is so full of castles that this pile of rubble scarcely seems to merit a second look. Yet this castle, which is now in a dangerous state, was at the centre of a cruel and bloody clan feud which would decide who controlled Cowal.

The ruin of Toward Castle stands near Toward Point, the southernmost tip of one of the four fingers which comprise the Cowal Peninsula. The castle was a stronghold of the Lamonts, who held sway over Cowal until the Campbells started to encroach.

In 1645, the Lamonts laid waste to Campbell land at Kilmun, and a year later the Campbells decided to retaliate. With a large force, the Campbells besieged the Lamonts in their castles of Toward and Ascog. They persuaded the Lamonts to surrender, on the condition that no lives would be taken. The Campbells broke their word, and the majority of Lamonts were either murdered or thrown into dungeons.

The walk begins at the Achafour Farm road end, on the A815 road about 1km from the eastern shore of

## INFORMATION

**Distance:** 7km (4.5 miles) one way: 14km (9 miles) return.

**Start:** Entrance to Achafour Farm, on A 815 road near Port Lamont.

**Finish:** Innellan.

Terrain: All on good farm and forestry roads or tracks. No special footwear needed.

**Public Transport:** Stagecoach Western Scottish bus services from Dunoon to Castle Toward (less frequently to Port Lamont).

**Refreshments:** Hotels and cafe at Innellan.

Yachts sail past lighthouse at Toward Point.

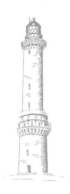

Loch Striven. To get there you travel south from Dunoon and pass Innellan, where the walk finishes.

You then continue on past Toward Point, and the lighthouse which has been virtually a final milestone for countless trippers who have sailed close by in steamers heading for Rothesay. When the sun strikes its white walls, the lighthouse glows like phosphorus against a background of fields and trees; and it is up behind those woods that this walk can be found.

From the Achafour Farm road end, walk to the farm then follow the unmetalled road north as it rises past fields and hedgerows. Looking back down this road, you see not only the lush local landscape, but also Rothesay, 'capital' of Bute, and the mountains of Arran further beyond. Here, in a glance, is the essence of Argyll: water, and wild moorland rich farmland existing side-by-side.

Above Achafour Farm, the view looks over to Rothesay on Bute and Arran beyond.

At Linne Mhor cottage you enter the wood, which at this point is mainly larch. As you continue, you see the eastern flank of Kilmarnock Hill, covered extensively in young trees. When you come to a Y-junction, keep on the direction you have been going, ignoring the right fork.

Away to the south, well out of sight, is another landmark worth mentioning. This is Castle Toward, an imposing Gothic mansion which can be seen from the decks of Rothesay ferries. It should not be confused with Toward Castle!

Castle Toward was built in 1820 for Kirkman Finlay, a Glasgow cotton magnate who became Lord Provost of the city. In the late 1940s, Glasgow Corporation bought the property as a centre where ailing slum boys could recover their health, and later it became an outdoor residential school where thousands of youngsters got their first taste of hillwalking, canoeing and other sports.

This walk gives an indication of how well placed Castle Toward was for its educational role. In 1996, when local government reorganisation took place in Scotland, the school became one of several outdoor centres that new councils could not afford to run. At the time of writing, its staff were intending to run the school independently.

Meanwhile back at the walk, you soon pass a stand of mature conifers felled by a gale. The forestry road heads downhill, past an old sand and gravel pit. At the bottom of the hill, the road crosses the Corlarach Burn by a concrete bridge and swings left uphill. Climbing the brae, you can see Loch Striven and the island of Bute.

Near the top of the brae, branch right along a forestry road which heads east, parallel to the burn. This is the road that leads to Innellan. It twists and turns up the glen, and over to the right you see a dry stone dyke separating Achafour Hill and Toward Hill. The road then swings downhill, towards the northeast, and passes another forestry road which branches uphill to the left.

Less than 300m further on you cross a concrete bridge to reach open wetland containing a pond. This pretty, peaceful spot seems miles from any habitation, but soon after you leave its intimacy, you are cresting the road and confronting the tower of the (currently mothballed) Inverkip power station across the Firth of Clyde.

As you descend steeply towards Innellan, you may see ferries plying back and forth across the firth, and the rounded hump of Ailsa Craig appears off the Ayrshire coast to the south. The road swings past areas where large conifers have been harvested then enters more woodland, popular for family walks.

Secluded pond.

You join Innellan at Wyndham Road, take a sharp right down Pier Road and arrive at the shore beside the derelict wooden pier.

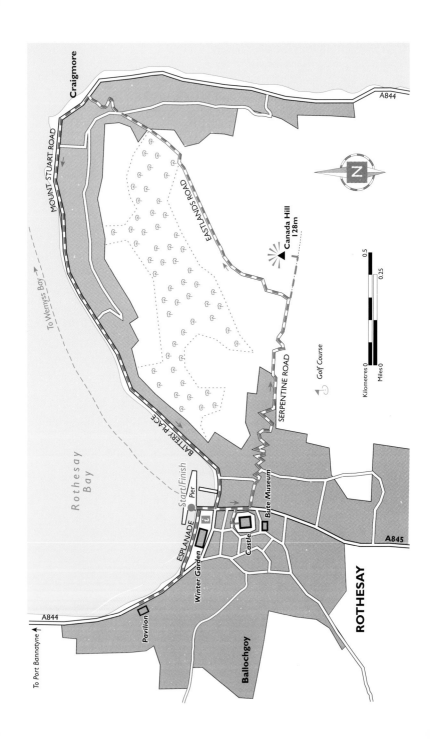

# ROTHESAY TOWN WALK

I s everything in the trunk? Too late if it's not, the steamer won't wait for ever at the Broomielaw just for the likes of us.

For well over a century, this was the moment that thousands of families longed for each year. The moment maw, paw and the weans would turn their backs on home and go *doon the watter* from the Glasgow area to holiday on the Firth of Clyde.

One of the most popular destinations was Rothesay, royal burgh and 'capital' of the Island of Bute. The last two titles probably didn't mean much to visitors who filled Rothesay's boarding houses or sought overspill accommodation in nearby Skeoch Woods. To them the town meant fresh air and seaside for the kids, and ligh-hearted entertainment for the grown-ups.

Rothesay may have been usurped long ago by foreign resorts, but it still retains a faded splendour. If the approach by sea is still stunning, imagine what it was like for families escaping from the fog, grime and disease of a Victorian Glasgow?

Visitors still stare fixedly towards Rothesay as their ferry passes Toward Point, the southern tip of the Cowal Peninsula. As the boat rounds Bogany Point, at the south end of Rothesay Bay, the town opens in an arc, with wooded hills behind.

Passengers first encounter the pier building, a small but stylish reminder of the Edwardian building destroyed by fire in 1962. Rothesay is believed to have had the Firth of Clyde's oldest recorded quay, in the 11th century, but its growth, like that of many Firth communities, stemmed from the explosion in steamer traffic in the 1800s.

To the right, dominating the Esplanade and surrounded by flower beds and putting greens, is the Winter Garden. Many of Scotland's greatest music hall artists performed in variety shows in this domed, steel and glass

## INFORMATION

**Distance:** 2km (1.5 miles).

**Terrain:** Pavements; steep steps up Serpentine Road.

**Public Transport:** Ferries from Wemyss Bay.

**Refreshments:** Wide choice.

The Rothesay coat of arms decorating a lamp post.

building. Saved recently from possible demolition, the Winter Garden still presents family shows.

Other sources of more than just wet-weather enjoyment are found deeper into the town. Bute Museum, behind the massive, red sandstone bulk of Rothesay Castle, has fascinating exhibits of pottery and other relics taken from ancient burial sites, as well as photographs of old steamers and natural history displays.

Visitors enter ruined Rothesay Castle by the front gate, unlike the Norwegians who hacked their way through the stone wall to force entry in 1230. Norwegian influence in Scotland ended in 1263 when King Haakon died following the Battle of Largs on the mainland opposite Bute.

Impressive Rothesay Castle surrounded by its moat.

The castle, with its huge, circular curtain wall, was also damaged by other forces including Cromwell's soldiers and the Campbells. One of Scotland's most important castles, it was repaired by the second Marquess of Bute in the early 1800s. A grimmer-looking building by far is the old Sheriff Court building nearby. This bleak, castellated piece of Victorian architecture seems more suited to executions than fines for breach of the peace.

For an outstanding view over the rooftops, walk west from the castle along Castle Street, then climb up Serpentine Road. This steep zigzag eventually leads up to Canada Hill, from where many people watched as emigrant ships took loved ones away from Scotland. Now it is a golf course. Returning to the bay, walk along Battery Place and Mount Stuart Road to admire some of the flamboyant old buildings on the front, particularly Glendale, with large bow windows and turreted roof.

Looking back to the terminal with its cluster of yachts tied up, and ferries coming to and fro, it is hard to imagine the volume of traffic that existed, say, in the mid-1800s. More than 20,000 Glasgow Fair holidaymakers would arrive in one day. The route from Glasgow became so competitive that rival steamer captains would goad each other into races. The fastest time for the 40-mile journey was 2 hours 28 minutes achieved by the *Rothesay Castle* in 1861.

Rothesay, "*This Venus rising out of the sea*", was not without its critics, however. One writer in the 1840s noted: "There is around the bay such an utter absence of bathing-apparatus, combined with natural want of facilities for privacy and due decorum, as would quite amaze any person accustomed to the bathing-places of England, or the east coast of Scotland".

Mount Stuart Road is named after the extravagant Gothic mansion, a few miles out of town, which is the seat of the Marquesses of Bute. The former racing driver, Johnny Dumfries, who won the 1988 Le Mans 24-hour race in a Jaguar, inherited the title and opened Mount Stuart to the public in 1995.

There is much more to see in Rothesay, notably the Pavilion, celebrated not only for its variety shows but also for its 1930s architecture. No male visitor should leave without investigating the town's Victorian toilets beside the terminal. The gentlemans' lavatory, all gleaming copper and ceramic, was restored at a cost of £300,000 and opened by a woman, Lucinda Lambton, the joyously eccentric architectural writer, in 1994.

The drones are tuned with an electronic meter as the Glasgow Skye Association pipe band get ready for the Rothesay Highland Games.

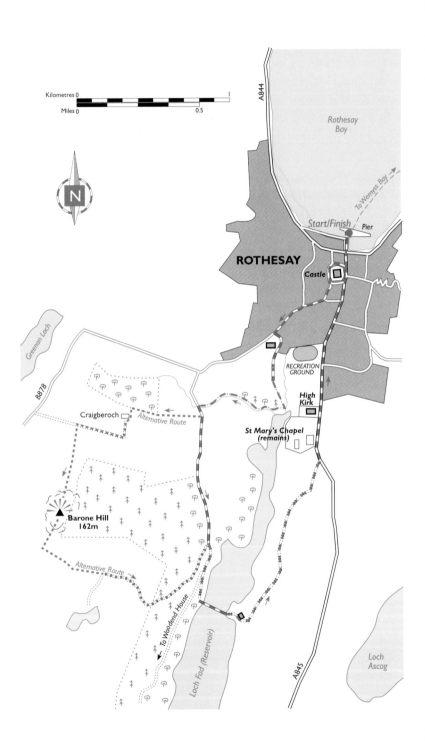

Kilometres 0                              1
Miles 0                        0.5

N

A844

Rothesay
Bay

To Wemyss Bay

Start/Finish    Pier

ROTHESAY

Castle

Greenan Loch

B878

RECREATION
GROUND

Craigberoch        Alternative Route

High
Kirk

St Mary's Chapel
(remains)

Barone Hill
162m

Alternative Route

To Woodend House

Loch Fad (Reservoir)

A845

Loch
Ascog

# LOCH FAD

The Island of Bute has been described as 'Scotland in miniature', with hilly moorland to the north and rich farmland to the south. This split is caused by the Highland Boundary Fault, a break in the earth's crust which creates a north-south divide between hard, mica schist rock and soft, red sandstone. The fault runs from Stonehaven in the north-east and passes through Loch Lomond before cutting Bute in two, from Rothesay to Scalpsie Bay.

Along this line runs a trench filled by Loch Fad, a reservoir popular for fly fishing. The walk to Loch Fad can be extended by 90 minutes or so by climbing Barone Hill, overlooking the town.

## INFORMATION

**Distance:** 5km (3.1 miles) for shorter, normal route. 7km (4.4 miles) including more arduous Barone Hill ascent. Add a further1km to see Kean's bust.

**Start and Finish:** Rothesay harbour.

**Terrain:** Good paths and tarmac roads for normal route. Stout footwear needed for rougher paths and grassy slope to Barone Hill.

**Public Transport:** CalMac ferries from Wemyss Bay.

**Refreshments:** Wide choice in Rothesay.

Waiting for a tug on the line, Loch Fad.

From Rothesay pier, join the High Street, passing Rothesay Castle, then turn right into Stuart Street, then on to Mill Street and Barone Road. At a gas depot, turn left into Meadows Road. Go through the recreation ground past tennis courts to a wooden gangway across the lade, the watercourse from Loch Fad which met increasing demand for water from the town's cotton mills.

In the mid 19th century, one mill alone employed about 360 people. Extra water was fed into Loch Fad by cuts, or channels, planned by the famous water engineer, Robert Thom.

Turn right, away from the High Kirk cemetery, and follow the path by Thom's Lovers' Walk Cut. You can still see water flowing down the cut as you join it at the Kirk Dam at the north end of Loch Fad. Follow the cut about 500m east, through a beech wood and pasture until you come to the tarmac road heading left to Barone Park Farm. Go past the farm for about 600m until you reach a three-way split in the road where the tarmac ends.

Alternatively, to climb Barone Hill, follow the tarmac road for about 50m then go through a gate into a field on your right. Follow a track up to a wood. Continue up through the trees and go through a small gate which leads onto a track leading uphill with mature trees on your right.

Soon you will see derelict Craigberoch farm to the left. At the farm is a standing stone with faint bronze age cup marks. Walk through the farm courtyard and turn left onto a tractor track. This soon swings right towards Barone Hill. Follow the track until it is about to drop to Greenan Loch. Go left through a gate and follow the fence down the field to a stile which takes you onto the hill.

The ascent is easy but avoid rocky outcrops. The summit view is worth the detour, taking in a panorama of Bute and neighbouring islands. This hill gave refuge to Rothesay people after the town was attacked in 1334 by Edward Balliol, seeking the Scottish throne with English help. It is also said that townsfolk rushed to the hill in fright after seeing smoke from the water. This was the Clyde's first steamship *Comet* on her maiden voyage in 1812.

From the summit, follow the stone dyke downhill for about 200m then cross it at a stile. A track heads down towards a water plant and a metalled road which leads to the three-way junction.

The middle road leads to Woodend House, built in 1824 as a retreat for the famous Shakespearean actor, Edmund Kean. Kean found shelter here from the scandal attached to his wild living in London: shock at his performing drunk on stage, or being sued for adultery. On Bute he did not scorn the bottle, but he enjoyed a quieter life, often casting a fly on Loch Fad.

Kean held a fireworks display for the island when busts of himself, Shakespeare, the dramatist Philip

The theatrical busts at the entrance to Woodend House.

Massinger and the actor David Garrick were unveiled at the estate entrance. Only nine years after arriving on Bute, Kean died, but the busts remain on their pillars, marking the end of public access on that road.

At the triple junction, take the road which drops down to a causeway which cuts across Loch Fad. This causeway provides a striking view of the hills of Arran. Loch Fad is stocked with trout which are caught from the banks, or from rowing boats which can be hired.

On Lover's Walk Cut.

Cross the causeway, pass the bailiff's hut and head back towards Rothesay. A farm road takes you to the main A845 road, which goes south to the beautiful Scalpsie and Kilchattan bays.

Returning to the harbour, you pass the ruined St Mary's Chapel beside the High Kirk, built in 1796. The church grounds contain the Bute family mausoleum, and the graves of Robert Thom and Napoleon's niece, Stephanie Hortense, who, like Kean, also came to Bute to find peace. Ironically, Battery Place, on the front, was named after cannons placed to ward off possible attack by her uncle's navy.

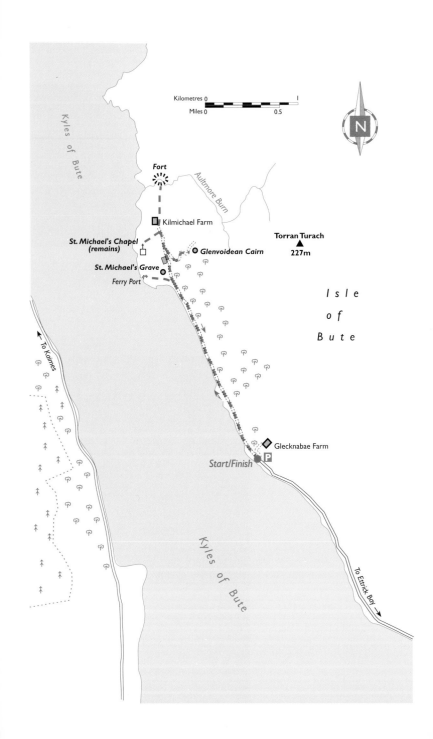

Kilometres 0 | 1
Miles 0 | 0.5

N

*Kyles of Bute*

Fort

*Aultmore Burn*

Kilmichael Farm

St. Michael's Chapel
(remains)

*Glenvoidean Cairn*

**Torran Turach**
▲
227m

St. Michael's Grave

*Ferry Port*

*I s l e*

*o f*

*B u t e*

*To Kaimes*

Glecknabae Farm

*Start/Finish* P

*Kyles of Bute*

*To Ettrick Bay*

# KILMICHAEL, BUTE

### INFORMATION

**Distance:** 5km (3 miles).

**Start and finish:** Parking area at entrance to Glecknabae Farm on Bute.

**Terrain:** Good farm roads. Short, easy scramble over shore rocks. Muddy track if you decide to visit fort site.

**Refreshments:** Cafe at Ettrick Bay.

Open any map for Cowal and Bute and you will find history trying to dominate the local geography. Every other farm seems to have its own stone circle, every hilltop its fort.

Neolithic man, Irish saints, Norse raiders, and Gaelic-speaking Highlanders have all left their mark in varying forms from physical landmarks to place-names. This walk, like so many others in the book, will fascinate anyone with a sense of the past and an eye for beautiful landscape. Its location should not be confused with the other, equally fascinating Kilmichael south of Oban in Argyll.

The walk can begin at Ettrick Bay, the lovely, sandy bay on the western side of Bute, popular with holidaymakers. Cars can, however, be driven a further 4km along a minor road and left in a parking area at the entrance to Glecknabae farm.

From the farm entrance, follow an unmetalled road north for about 1km until a track leads left towards the shore. Follow this down to the shingle beach and then start scrambling across easy rocks to a tiny inlet. This was the site of a ferry which once provided a link across the Kyles of Bute to the village of Kames on the mainland. The ferry is long gone, as are the large numbers of fishing boats which used to sail out of Bute in search of herring and haddock.

As you return to the road, you will see in the field up to your left a cluster of large stones. This is a chambered cairn, called St Michael's Grave because it is near the chapel dedicated to an Irish saint, Macaille. The cairn belongs to the Neolithic period, which is dated roughly between 4000-2000BC. This was the final stage of the stone age when humans gave up the precarious existence of being hunter-gatherers and ensured for themselves a greater chance of survival through farming and domesticating animals.

These settlers came to Scotland by sea as the terrain - mountainous, boggy and heavily forested - made cross-country travel extremely arduous. Bute, sitting at a maritime crossroads, became a natural destination for these early settlers.

What remains of the cairn are flat stone slabs which formed the cist or chest within which some burnt bones and flints, believed to come from Arran, were found in the early 1900s. The large capping stone lies on the ground.

Glenvoidean cairn, looking south towards Arran.

It wasn't until the 1960s that an older and more elaborate cairn was recognised by Mrs D. B. Taylor on land also belonging to Kilmichael farm, a few hundred metres uphill from St Michael's Grave. Carbon dating has shown that the cairn, the Glenvoidean cairn, could be as much as 5,000 years old.

To reach it, return to the farm road, turn left and go past the cottage. About 100 metres further on, take a track that rises back up the hill above the cottage. Go through a gate that has to be slid open and continue up the track. Walk past trees and look about 200m uphill to see the top of the cairn touching the skyline.

Glenvoidean was excavated by Mrs Taylor and Miss Dorothy N. Marshall, who have written the *History of Bute*, a fascinating and detailed guide to the history and archaeology of Bute. The two women were assisted by fellow members of the Buteshire Natural History Society, which has produced an excellent series of walking guides.

Glenvoidean cairn, looking across the Kyles of Bute to Kames.

The layout of the stones, with the two largest

forming a V thrusting into the sky, reveals a series of distinct chambers built over a long period of time. The discovery that Glenvoidean was in use over several periods makes it particularly important archaeologically. It is hard not to be moved by the cairn and its situation. Here, in the middle of a field overlooking the Kyles of Bute with views to mainland Argyll, Arran and Kintyre, is a structure that was being created at the same time as the pyramids of Egypt.

Cast iron headstones from 1890s graveyard of St Michael's Chapel.

Continue towards Kilmichael farm. Before the farm, turn left through a gate in a dyke and go down a field, following a fence towards the Kyles. Go through the gate which leads into a second field, in which you will see the ruin of St Michael's Chapel. Walk slowly as there may be livestock, and enter the chapel grounds through an old iron gate. Inside the ruin is a stone slab, which was the altar, and a recess in a wall which would have held church vessels. The graveyard was used by the villagers of Kames.

The walk can be continued to the site of a fort, just beyond Kilmichael farm. There is not much to see as the site has not been excavated, but it can be reached by walking through the farm, and continuing about 200 metres along a track bordered by farm machinery. As this is a tractor track, it can be very muddy. The fort is on the bank of the Aultmore burn. Go through a sliding gate before the burn, and then right for a few yards to the site, a mound in an angle of the burn.

Return to the start by the outward route.

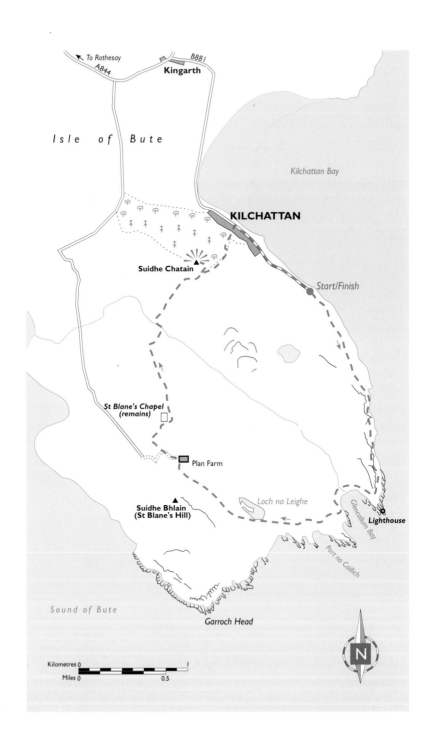

To Rothesay
A844
B881
Kingarth

Isle of Bute

Kilchattan Bay

KILCHATTAN

Suidhe Chatain

Start/Finish

St Blane's Chapel
(remains)

Plan Farm

Suidhe Bhlain
(St Blane's Hill)

Loch na Leighe

Glencallum Bay

Port na Caillich

Lighthouse

Sound of Bute

Garroch Head

Kilometres 0 ........ 1
Miles 0 ........ 0.5

N

# KILCHATTAN BAY, BUTE

This circular walk near the southern tip of Bute has many attractions. It incudes a shoreline path passing strange rock formations, a ruined 12th century chapel on the site of a Celtic monastery, and a hill with an outstanding view over the sands of Kilchattan Bay and the starting point, the village of Kilchattan.

Kilchattan (pronounced with the 'h' silent) has a frontage of red sandstone villas looking across the Firth of Clyde to the island of Arran. Old red sandstone is something you will see a lot of as you head south to a kissing gate giving access to the path above the shore. Although this popular route is not a right of way, access is granted by the landowner, the Marquess of Bute.

From the kissing gate, follow the path through rough grassland. The path partly hugs the side of steep cliffs. At one point, a prominent outcrop of red sandstone seems to teeter overhead. This outcrop was carved into weird shapes by waves when the land was lower and the sea higher than now. Ridges of molten basalt can

## INFORMATION

**Distance:** 7km (4.4 miles).

**Start and finish:** Kilchattan village, Bute.

**Terrain:** Mainly tracks, boggy for short stretches. Farm roads for short distance. No special footwear needed.

**Public** Transport: Stagecoach Western Scottish buses to Kilchattan from Rothesay. Train from Glasgow Central to Wemyss Bay for Caledonian MacBrayne ferry to Rothesay.

**Refreshments:** Hotel at Kilchattan.

Approaching red sandstone cliffs near the start of the walk.

also be seen on the shoreline. Out to sea, you may spot a seal sticking its nose up for air, or cormorants flying past on the hunt for fish. Background sounds of wind and water may be broken by the noise of engines, as cargo boats head through the firth.

About 2km from the start, you reach the lighthouse on a rocky promontory at Glencallum Bay. At the

Lighthouse at Glencallum Bay.

innermost part of the bay, about 200m from the shore, boulders are the only remains of an old inn. Here, crews awaiting a fair wind for North America and other destinations got their last refreshment before setting sail.

The route continues over the ridge at the west side of the bay. Head for a scattering of boulders, then follow a track through bracken up to a cleft in the ridge. The track passes above some small bays including Port na Caillich, the *port of the old woman*. After the second bay the track climbs to higher ground.

Ahead you will see four ridges running into the sea. Head round the curving hillside and make for the hill at the top of the second ridge. When you reach the top, you find yourself looking down on a beautiful, private corner. This is Loch na Leighe, a rich haunt of birdlife turned green by water lilies and bullrushes growing in the water.

At the lowest part of the ridge, overlooking the loch, is a small cave. From the loch, a track leads off to the left and joins an old farm road to Plan Farm. Go past the front of the farmhouse and turn left onto a road which soon passes a field on the right. Cross the field and go through a kissing gate beside a stone wall. Follow the wall uphill to St Blane's Chapel, on a grassy mound among trees. Though a ruin, much of this building remains, particularly the Norman arch, which has chevrons cut into the stonework.

The site, protected by Historic Scotland, is thought to have become a centre of Christian worship in the late 6th century when St Catan, who was born in Ireland, established a monastery (thus Kilchattan, the cell or chapel of Catan). According to belief, St Catan's sister Ertha became pregnant by an unknown man and as a punishment she and her baby, the future St Blane, were cast adrift in an oarless boat which landed in Ireland. After being educated by Saints Kenneth and Comgall, Blane returned to Bute and succeeded his uncle as abbot.

St Blane moved to the mainland and founded what was to become Dunblane Cathedral, north of Stirling. Meanwhile on Bute, Vikings are believed to have destroyed the monastery in the late 8th century. A Viking hogback gravestone is in the graveyard. Catan is also remembered at sites on Colonsay, Islay and Jura. The chapel and its surrounds retain a monastic tranquillity. The site warrants some time for quiet exploration before leavng for the next stretch of the walk.

To rejoin the walk, leave the chapel grounds by the small, iron entrance gate. Turn right and go through a gap in the cashel or boundary wall and go straight ahead, past a stone base with a socket which once held a wooden cross. Go through a gate and head leftwards, uphill past farm ruins. Over the rise, go down to where two fences meet. Follow the right-hand fence downhill. Up on the left, with a radio tower on its flank, is Suidhe Chatain (Catan's seat), on the route.

Follow the fence as it turns left at the bottom of the hill and reaches a bridge, crossing a stream in boggy Branzet Moss. Cross the fence leading up to Suidhe Chatain and head uphill. Just before you reach another fence leading in from the left, go through a gate on your right and continue uphill. Follow the fence past Suidhe Chatain until you reach a gate. Climb to the summit, crossing a second fence by a stile, then through a gap in a dyke. The summit has wonderful views over a large area of Bute as well as Glen Sannox and Goat Fell on Arran.

Return to the gate, then go downhill towards Kilchattan, keeping bracken to your left. Lower down, make for a stone wall on the left and go through a kissing gate at the left-hand corner of the field. Follow the track by the wall, then, just above Kilchattan, go through a kissing gate into the wood. The track continues through the wood to the rear of houses, and becomes a lane which takes you to the shore front beside a telephone box, only 200m north of the pier.

*Opposite:* The carved Norman arch of St Blane's Chapel.

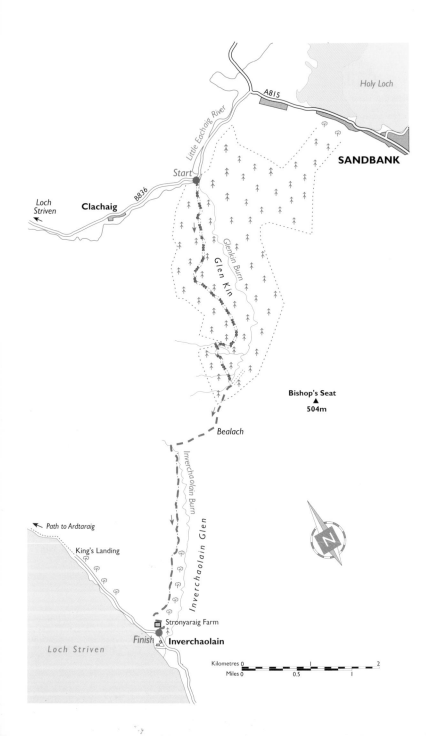

# THE COFFIN ROAD

It is little more than 100 years ago, the blinking of an eye, that the first petrol-driven automobiles took to the roads. Before that historical moment and for some time after, people living in areas of rough terrain could only travel by boat, on horseback or on foot.

Through necessity, people in the Highlands had literally to take distance in their stride. Part of the network of long distance paths was formed by coffin roads. Those paths were used to carry Highlanders in their coffins to the graveyard of their home district. On these journeys, local men would take turns to carry the coffins. At points along the route, cairns would be built to rest the heavy loads and to mark the way.

The coffin road described here stretches from Glen Kin, north-west of Dunoon, to Inverchaolain, on the eastern shore of Loch Striven. Inverchaolain has a church and graveyard in a beautiful setting. Although this may have been the last destination of many of the coffins and their occupants which were borne over the pass of Bealach na Sreine, it has also been suggested that after the Reformation, Episcopalians would have been carried in the opposite direction, from Inverchaolain to the cemetery at Kilmun.

The walk begins on the B836 road, less than 1km east of Clachaig village, which was the site of a gunpowder factory from 1839 to 1905. If you are heading from

## INFORMATION

**Distance:** 7.6km (4.75 miles) one way.

**Start:** Glen Kin, 1km east of Clachaig Village. Turn left from A885 4km north of Dunoon onto B836 and continue for 2km to the bridge over the Glenkin Burn.

**Finish:** Inverchaolain, on the east bank of Loch Striven.

**Terrain:** Good forest roads, grassy hillside, hill track. Boots not necessary, though walking trainers or stout shoes advised. Map and compass should be taken, but the route should not be attempted in bad visibility.

**Public Transport:** None to the start or finish. Stagecoach Western Scottish buses and Postbus services to and from Dunoon on B836. Limited Stagecoach Western Scottish bus service from Dunoon to Port Lamont, 3km south of Inverchaolain.

**Refreshments;** None en route - take food and drink with you. Nearest refreshments in Dunoon.

On the forestry road.

Dunoon, turn left into the trees just before the bridge over the Glenkin Burn. Go through a gate which leads to a forestry road. Here, a sign asks you to fasten all gates, keep to the path, not to light fires, take all litter home and keep dogs under control. Please comply.

The slowly winding uphill stretch through the plantation lasts for just over 1km. On the way there may be warning signs about timber harvesting, and requests to keep off stacked timber. Watch out for any timber lorries coming round the bends. From the plantation there is a fine view of the western flank of Bishop's Seat, the hill which overlooks Dunoon and is covered in Walk 13. Further on, where conifers have been cleared, a mixture of oak and ash saplings are growing in plastic tubes to protect them from the weather and grazing animals.

In the upper section of the plantation you can see the ridge formed by Leacann nan Gall and Green Knap descending from the right to the bealach (pass or gap). Shortly after you see the bealach, the road takes a U-turn to the left and heads back down the glen, following the opposite bank of the burn. At this bend, the road crosses two streams. Beside the second stream, there is a small cairn on the right-hand side of the road. An arrow on the boulders points to a path up the left-hand bank of the second stream. Take care not to miss this turnoff.

Follow the path up through an attractive birchwood until you reach a fence which is crossed by a stile. Here there is the macabre ornament of a sheep's skull bound to a fence-post by barbed wire.

On the track to Stronyaraig Farm and Loch Striven.

There is no distinct path up the grassy slope to the Bealach na Sreine, but the route is straightforward. Head uphill past a large rowan tree, and trend gradually right until you reach a point where three fences meet. From here, the ground falls away to the lush and wooded floor of the glen. Running through the glen is the Inverchaolain Burn, which flows into Loch Striven beyond.

The cairn at the top of the climb, looking down into Inverchaolain Glen.

When you start to go downhill, look out for a small cairn which would appear to have been used by coffin bearers, resting after a hard climb to the bealach. Continue down the western side of the glen, and head for a sheepfank (walled enclosure) near the head of the burn.

The way is tussocky but never difficult. As you get close to the burn, aim for an easy crossing about 300m below the sheepfank. Once across the burn, you join a track which continues down the glen for 3km to Stronyaraig Farm and the end of the walk. The path can be wet and muddy in places, but otherwise the surface is good enough to let you admire the scenery as you walk.

At Stronyaraig Farm, the route, which is now a right of way, continues past the sheep dip and farm buildings to the main road at Inverchaolain.

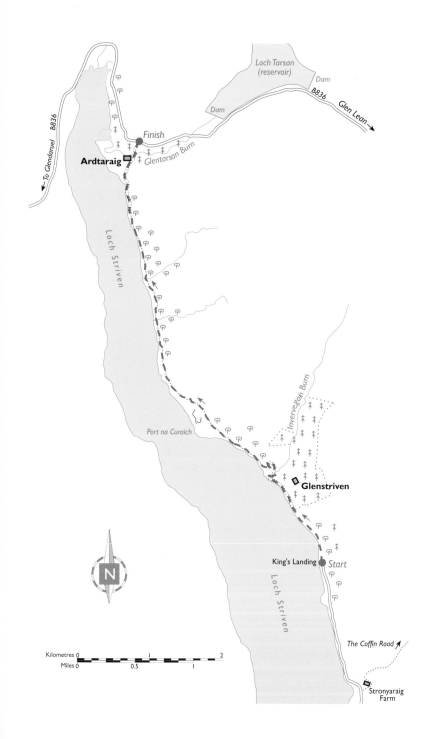

Loch Tarsan
(reservoir)

Dam

B836    Glen Lean

To Glendaruel    B836

Dam

*Finish*

**Ardtaraig**    Glentarsan Burn

Loch Striven

Invervegan Burn

Port na Curaich

**Glenstriven**

King's Landing    *Start*

Loch Striven

N

The Coffin Road

Kilometres 0          1          2
Miles 0        0.5        1

Stronyaraig
Farm

# LOCH STRIVEN

The Cowal Peninsula looks like a four-fingered hand that is trying to grasp the Island of Bute. The biggest stretch of water separating any two of those fingers is Loch Striven.

This sea loch reveals a sharp contrast along its 10km length. At its southern end, beside acres of rich farmland, lies Ardyne Point, where an oil production yard was built in the 1970s. A short distance further north is a NATO fuel depot, which has oil storage tanks on the hill above the jetty to service naval ships. The shores along much of this beautiful loch's northern section, however, are relatively unspoiled and hilly.

The walk described here follows part of the east shoreline from Glenstriven to Ardtaraig at the head of the loch. The route can be combined with the Coffin

## INFORMATION

**Distance:** 7km (4.5miles) one way; 14km (9 miles) return.

**Start:** Glenstriven. From Dunoon take A815 south to Toward and then continue for 16km on narrow minor road to Glenstriven.

**Finish:** Ardtaraig, on B836.

**Terrain:** Good farm road followed by path which goes through thickets and stretches of very boggy ground. Water-repellent footwear or wellingtons recommended.

**Public transport:** None to start and finish. Two cars will be needed unless the route is to be reversed, in which case its length is doubled.

**Refreshments:** None en route. Take food and drink with you.

Evening sunlight on the loch.

Road (Walk 19), to make a long but interesting day, using the B836 road for the start and finish.

The walk begins at King's Landing, at the entrance to Glenstriven Estate, about 2km north of Inverchaolain (the finish for the Coffin Road). A Scottish Rights of Way Society signpost, beside the estate lodge, indicates the footpath to Ardtaraig. The path is initially overshadowed by trees, rhododendrons and beautiful wild fuchsia. The route crosses a stream then joins a farm road, which continues heading north, at one point passing a house then fording a river by a wooden bridge.

As you walk along, you may be getting a feeling that you are not alone. Out on the loch, almost constantly visible, is the liquid gas tanker, the *LNG Lagos*. As a notice at the start of the walk explains, the Lagos was built in 1976 and has not

Mothballed gas tanker, the *LNG Lagos,* at anchor in the loch.

done a day's work in her life. Apart from a period of dry docking, she has been mothballed, awaiting a call from Shell. Meanwhile, a crew of three remain on board to maintain her machinery.

The road beyond the wooden bridge appears to be a recent extension to the estate network. The road goes uphill and comes to a fork. Take the left branch, indicated by an arrow painted on a slate. About 400m from here is a stand of young ash trees. As you approach Port na Curaich, jutting into the loch, another slate arrow indicates the road you take over the point.

Take a last look down the loch before joining the old path which heads north along the shore. You join the path where the estate road swings right in a U-bend. This path is very boggy in parts, but is much more attractive because of its relative naturalness. The path occasionally splits, as you walk through rhododendrons, heather and silver birch, but its various branches always meet up again, so there is no real danger of going astray.

Soon you descend a hillside of bracken to a rocky beach. If you walk quietly you might spot gulls and other birds on a rock outcrop littered with shells which the birds have smashed to extract the contents.

This part of the shore is particularly beautiful, especially on a still summer's evening when birds can be heard calling across the water. Loch Striven might have been on the mind of Lord Cockburn, the famous judge and diarist who wrote in 1838: "The whole of these Argyleshire sea lochs are glorious. The boldness and beauty of their scenery, their strange, savage history..."

Bee attracted to a thistle.

Lord Cockburn could be brutal about Scottish places and manners but his love of Argyll was not in doubt. He summed up one idyllic day thus: "So we just sauntered by the shore, and talked, and gathered shells, and skiffed flat stones on the surface of the sea, and sat on rocks and lay on the turf, and played with the clear water, and gazed, unceasingly gazed, on the hills, and watched the shadows of the clouds, and observed how the prospects varied with our positions, and with the progress of the sun, and in short had a long luxurious day of repose and enjoyment."

The walk continues for a short spell across grass then settles into a steady succession of tree thickets and boggy ground where streams have to be crossed. When you start to come past a series of rock overhangs on the right, you are nearing the final stages of the walk.

The going underfoot improves once you go through an old iron gate in a dyke and join a farm road. This road takes you past a small bay and slipway and the sombrely elegant Ardtaraig House, with its crow-stepped gables. Go through the adjacent farm courtyard and follow the estate road as it twists up through trees to the B836.

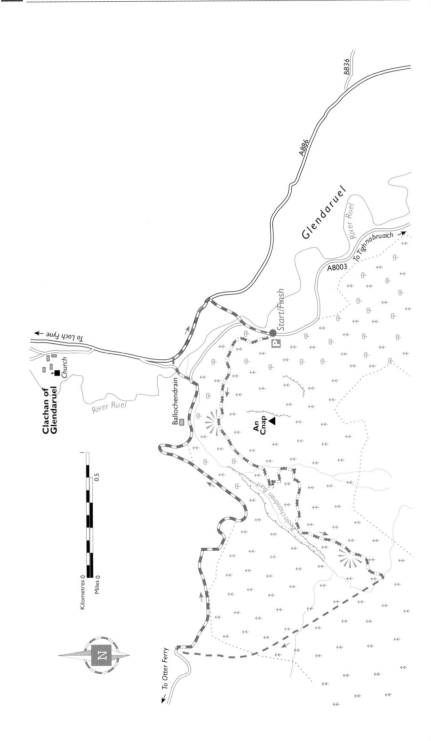

Clachan of
Glendaruel

Church

River Ruel

Ballochendrain

An
Cnap

Bealach-an-druim Burn

Glendaruel

River Ruel

A8003
To Tighnabruaich →

A886

B836

Start/Finish

To Loch Fyne

To Otter Ferry

Kilometres 0    0.5    1
Miles 0

N

# GLENDARUEL

lendaruel is a secret that maybe shouldn't be divulged. It has everything a lover of the countryside could ask for: beautiful, lush scenery, a long history, and the sea, as well as hill and forest walks on its doorstep.

Over the years, many people have passed through Glendaruel, including the Vikings, who paid the price for their visit by being slaughtered here around the year 1110. Yet recently a young French tourist was so surprised at how quiet the A886 main road from Strachur was that she asked the local campsite owner whether the road was private.

One reason why Glendaruel, and indeed much of Cowal, has everything but the crowds may be found in tourist maps, which tend to give a less than complete coverage of the area - even missing out important road links. All this may be fine for those already in on the Glendaruel secret, but it is not much help for those who would like to find out.

## INFORMATION

**Distance:** 8km (5 miles).

**Start and finish:** Forest track entrance beside A8003, about 800m south of A886 junction.

**Terrain:** Steep forestry road, possibly wetter underfoot on disused road section. Return by twisting, single track tarmac road. Boots recommended.

**Public transport:** Stagecoach Western Scottish bus services to Dunoon, Portavadie, Strachur or Colintraive for Bute ferry.

**Refreshments:** Glendaruel Hotel.

Looking down onto Clachan of Glendaruel from the forest road.

This mainly forest walk begins about 1km south of the small hamlet of Clachan of Glendaruel and gives an outstanding view of the community, with its attractive church and inn, as well as a large stretch of the glen to the north.

To reach the start, head south from the Clachan and turn right onto the A8003 road to Tighnabruaich.

After about 800m you reach the black gravel entrance to a forestry road. There is room to park beside this entrance.

Kilmodan Church.

Head up the forest road through mixed woodland. As you climb you can see the bare top of An Cnap up to the left. Higher up the road, a break in the trees reveals the Clachan, dominated by Kilmodan Church. St Modan was a Celtic saint, living at the same time as St Columba, who set up a chapel in the glen. He is said to have lived beside Loch Etive for a time and also at both Falkirk, where he founded a church, and Rosneath on the Clyde, where he died. In the graveyard at Kilmodan is an enclosure containing carved gravestones from the 15th and 16th centuries.

The road continues up past a small waterfall and eventually over a culvert. Through this flows the Bealachandrain Burn that flows down into a gorge below the road. The road then twists round a bend where rocks have been blasted to clear the way.

Go past an area of wind-blasted trees, and continue uphill for about 200m to cross a culvert. The road continues steeply uphill, passing above another small gorge to the main viewpoint overlooking Glendaruel.

After the viewpoint, the road zigzags uphill then descends for about 300m to a stream that goes through a culvert. This culvert is an important landmark as 40m further on, round a left-hand corner, you leave the road to join a disused forestry track on the right.

At the time of writing, this track looked like a firebreak because its entrance was blocked by fallen trees. The track heads north-west through the forest, eventually coming out onto a small stretch of open moorland at Cruach nan Tarbh (*bull hill*), then continues to the Ballochendrain road, between Glendaruel and Otter Ferry on Loch Fyne. The crest of this road was called the Place of Weeping, because it gave many people from the Highlands and Islands the last glimpse of their homeland before they headed for emigrant ships or the slums of Glasgow.

Although Argyll did not experience the large clearances which saw sheep replace people in Sutherland and Ross-shire, the collapse of the traditional Highland economy and clan system after the Battle of Culloden in 1746 forced large scale migration from the glens. In the1830s and 1840s, potato crop failures threatened famine on an Irish scale which was only averted by prompt charitable action.

The walk now leads down the Ballochendrain road, back to Glendaruel. Otter Ferry, by the way, does not refer to otters, but to *Oitir*, the Gaelic word for a sandy or shingle spit. It was here that the Vikings landed before making their ill-fated raid into Glendaruel. There is confusion over the origin of the glen's name. It is said the name originally contained *ruadh*, the Gaelic word for red, signifying the rust-coloured water in the River Ruel, but the river also became the 'bloody water', after the Vikings' bodies were thrown into it.

As you go down into the glen, watch out for vehicles as this attractive road is narrow and twisty. A shortcut back to the forestry road entrance cannot be used because a bridge over a stream has collapsed; continue on to the main A886 road then take the Tighnabruaich turnoff.

Bridge over the River Ruel at the bottom of the Ballochendrain road.

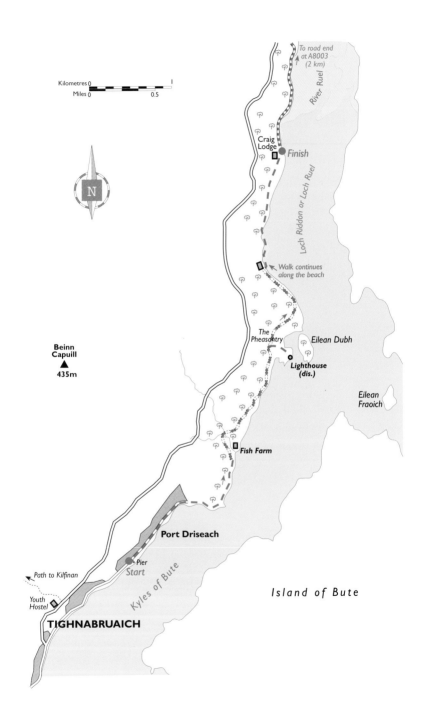

To road end
at A8003
(2 km)

River Ruel

Kilometres 0     1
Miles 0     0.5

N

Craig
Lodge

Finish

Loch Riddon or Loch Ruel

Walk continues
along the beach

The
Pheasantry

Eilean Dubh

Lighthouse
(dis.)

Beinn
Capuill
▲
435m

Eilean
Fraoich

Fish Farm

**Port Driseach**

Pier
Start

Kyles of Bute

Path to Kilfinan

*Island of Bute*

Youth
Hostel

**TIGHNABRUAICH**

# KYLES OF BUTE

There are some people who insist that the most famous person ever to have taken a boat through the Kyles of Bute never actually existed. They will argue that Peter Macfarlane was only the figment of some journalist's imagination, as was the boat itself, the *Vital Spark*.

Well maybe it's true, strictly speaking, that there never was such a Macfarlane, or Para Handy as he was better known. But Neil Munro, the native of Argyll who went on to edit a Glasgow evening newspaper, obviously knew many sailing men who were characters just as much as his fictional creation Para Handy, master of a puffer which was 'chust sublime'.

For centuries, people in Argyll had to rely on water rather than road for travel and supplies. The terrain was rough and roads themselves were few and far between until the Jacobite rebellions prompted a flurry of construction by Government troops.

The sea which brought the Scots from Ireland and the Vikings from Norway eventually became the main thoroughfare for the 19th century explosion in tourism. Communities like Tighnabruaich, where this walk begins, expanded to meet holiday demand. In

## INFORMATION

**Distance:** 8km (5 miles) from Tighnabruaich to the A8003. 12km (7.5 miles) from Tighnabruaich to Criag Lodge and back.

**Start:** Tighnabruaich.

**Finish:** Craig Lodge road end at A8003 road, about 8km north of Tighnabruaich.

**Terrain:** Good gravel road to halfway, then awkward scramble over boulders, and finally steep hillside tracks. Boots or strong shoes with cleated, rubber soles recommended.

**Public transport:** Stagecoach Western Scottish services from Tighnabruaich to Dunoon.

Autumn berries, looking across the Kyles of Bute.

doing so, they relied even more on coasters or puffers bringing supplies. In some places close to sandy beaches, locals would give their order for a year's coal and the puffer would run up onto the beach. The coal would be loaded onto farmers' carts and the puffer would pull away at high tide.

Tighnabruaich, a pretty village of whitewashed houses facing across the Kyles (narrows) of Bute to the Island of Bute, is still a popular holiday destination, as its youth hostel and sailing school confirm. This walk passes a stretch of the Kyles. These separate Bute from the mainland and are widely recognised as having some of the most beautiful coastal scenery in Scotland.

In the village, head north along the shore road past the marina then follow a forestry road which curves up the side of a cliff. The road follows the shore, passing a fish farm and at times overshadowed by rhododendron bushes which obscure the view.

The road continues, at one point crossing over a waterfall and then rising to a small viewpoint with a bench overlooking the water. Across the water on the Bute shore are the famous Maids of Bute, two rocks resembling women. According to *Para Handy Tales*, it was Para himself who had the decency to paint clothes on them.

Disused beacon beside
Eilean Dubh.

About 3km from the centre of the village you reach a particularly beautiful spot, known as the pheasantry. Here a disused lighthouse stands like a white, stone pepper pot on a rocky promontory opposite the small, wooded island of Eilean Dubh.

The road swings round to the north-west and reaches a farmhouse with a sign indicating the path to Ormidale

Ferry. At this point the walk becomes much more challenging as it takes to the beach, then continues on through woods and over rocks. Walk north along the beach, cross a stream and continue along the shore for about 200m until you see where a track goes into the wood. Follow the track to large table-topped boulders on the beach near a fish farm.

The nearest large boulder has a green arrow with 'footpath', pointing to the left. Here, you have to clamber awkwardly round behind the boulder, which may be slippery. Cross over a stream and clamber up behind more rocks then follow tapes and arrows which mark the track through the trees. Along the track you have to make yet another awkward manoeuvre, crossing a stream whose opposite bank is vertical and muddy. Look for handholds on the rock wall to your left.

The track soon gains height, giving a view of the fish farm. Along the way, rhododendrons have been cleared from the track, an old right-of-way. After a brief spell of lofty walking, with views over the Kyles, the track begins to descend towards Craig Lodge. The final stretch is a steep bank where care must be taken, otherwise you could almost literally land on the roof of this whitewashed, Victorian house.

Near the end of the walk: Craig Lodge.

The tarmac road from the lodge leads north for 2km to the main A8003 road, which provides outstanding viewpoints overlooking the Kyles of Bute.

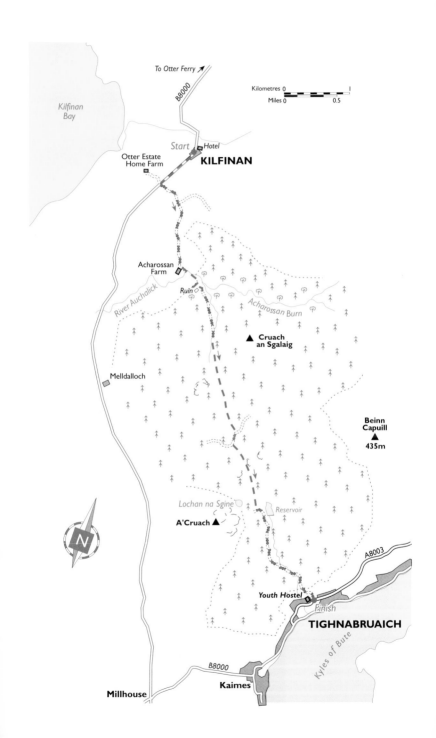

To Otter Ferry

B8000

Kilfinan Bay

Kilometres 0 — 1
Miles 0 — 0.5

Start — Hotel
**KILFINAN**

Otter Estate
Home Farm

Acharossan
Farm

River Auchalick

Ruin

Acharossan Burn

▲ Cruach
an Sgalaig

Melldalloch

Beinn
Capuill
▲
435m

Lochan na Sgine

Reservoir

A'Cruach ▲

N

A8003

Youth Hostel

Finish

**TIGHNABRUAICH**

Kyles of Bute

B8000

**Millhouse**

**Kaimes**

# KILFINAN TO TIGHNABRUAICH

Ten per cent of all conifers planted for industry in Britain are grown in Argyll. Over 150,000 hectares here are covered in spruce, larch and pine.

This walk is an old right of way which goes through one of Cowal's biggest stretches of woodland, starting and ending at an attractive village. You can start at Kilfinan, a tiny settlement beside Loch Fyne, and end at Tighnabruaich beside the Kyles of Bute.

Most of this walk is along firebreaks and tracks, but don't fear that you will be constantly hemmed by walls of dark green needles. There are hillocks which give outstanding views, and in the depths of the forest you may experience a peculiar sense of isolation that persuades you, possibly correctly, that you are the only person around.

From Kilfinan village (named for St Finnan, another Celtic saint), walk 500m south along the B8000 road and turn left into the farm road opposite the entrance to Otter Estate home farm. Follow the road through a gate where a sign says dogs must be kept on leads. The track soon swings south-east, the direction you will generally follow. Pass a road leading left and go through a second gate. Further on, ignore a track heading right; instead keep straight on, following an old track downhill, with bracken to the left and silver birches to the right.

## INFORMATION

**Distance:** 8km (5 miles).

**Start:** Kilfinan village.

**Finish:** Tighnabruaich.

**Terrain:** Farm roads, forestry firebreaks and tracks. Boots or wellingtons advised for boggy and muddy stretches.

**Public transport:** Bus service between Kilfinan and Tighnabruaich, run by Tighnabruaich Service Station and Portavadie Coach Hire.

**Refreshments:** Hotels at Kilfinan and Tighnabruaich.

*Left:* Muddy going through Acharossan Farm.

*Right:* The old wood beyond Acharossan Farm.

With electricity poles running alongside your left, cross an old gate then continue along a more obvious track until you see whitewashed Acharossan farmhouse. Go through the farmyard, avoiding the mud. From the yard, cross the River Auchalick by an old stone bridge then go through a galvanised steel gate ahead. Walk through an attractive, old woodland of Scots pines and beech trees, between the Acharossan Burn and a stone dyke. Cross a stile, follow the dyke on and then round a right-hand corner (where a barbed wire fence will be nearer you).

After about 50 metres you will see a white post at the edge of the plantation. Here, enter a clearing in the wood and head towards another post over to the left. In the trees to your right you may glimpse a small ruined building. Continue slanting left towards another white post and Stowhall Burn, which flows into Acharossan Burn. Follow the edge of the plantation south-east, above Stowhall Burn, and look for a white tape hanging from a tree, and yet another marker post.

Soon follow a firebreak uphill on a well-marked track. In a small clearing, where you can see the bare top of Cruach an Sgalaig to the east, come to a post. You can join another firebreak, in line with the one you came out of, or head left to Stowhall Burn which offers a more attractive route, with silver birch and rowan by its banks.

Following Stowhall Burn uphill, you soon meet the firebreak. Go quietly here and you may see deer. Continue up the firebreak, passing other breaks leading in from both sides, and reach level ground where you will find a marker post. Climbing slightly, cross a broken-down stone dyke and maintain the direction you have been taking, with the forest edge to your right.

Follow the track along the lowest ground, with trees to your right and a broad heather slope to your left. Go through a small gap in the trees, and the heather slope opens up again on the left. Curve to the right, still following the edge of the forest, then, leaving the heather slope, enter a new stretch of firebreak beside a fallen tree.

Signs in the depths of the forest.

Continue along this break, and see another post, and a heather slope again to your left. Pass over the watershed and go downhill, passing the entrance to a firebreak coming in from the right. Continuing along the firebreak, you can see the bare top of A'Chruach ahead. The firebreak comes down to a forestry road where a sign points back to Kilfinan and another indicates Tighnabruaich (the name means *house on the slope*). Turn right.

About 100m down the road you reach a similar set of signs where you turn left off the road to the plantation, where a post marks the start of another firebreak. In this break go over a small burn, then cut briefly north-east to where a second post leads deeper into the break. Go up a grassy firebreak for about 200m, then join another break joining from the right, indicated by another post.

Follow this break below the slopes of a 200m high hillock which you can climb to get a view of Lochan na Sgine, the Kyles of Bute and Loch Fyne. Below, at the end of the hillock, branch right where a post leads down yet another firebreak. The path gradually descends between a fence on the right, at the base of A'Chruach, and the plantation on the left.

At a post beside the fence, which leads to Lochan na Sgine, take the firebreak running off to the left. Do not follow the fence as it leads over tussocky, ankle-twisting ground.

More poles lead you along the firebreak to a clearing. Skirt left round the clearing's edge, passing a pole which may be hard to spot in the grass. Pass two more poles which mark the route out of the clearing and east to Tighnabruaich. The track becomes more obvious downhill, eventually quitting the conifers for Douglas firs and rhododendrons, until you arrive at Tighnabruaich, beside the youth hostel.

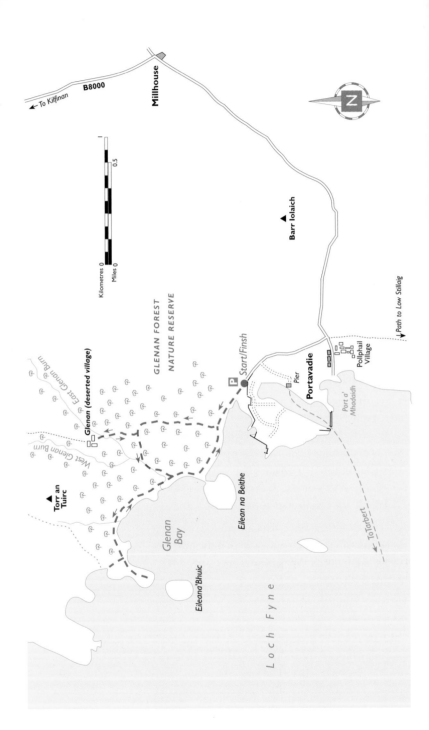

To Kilfinan

B8000

Millhouse

N

Barr Iolaich

Kilometres 0 0.5 1
Miles 0

GLENAN FOREST
NATURE RESERVE

East Glenan Burn

Glenan (deserted village)

West Glenan Burn

Torr an Tuirc

Start/Finish

P

Pier

Portavadie

Pollphail Village

Path to Low Stillaig

Eilean na Beithe

Port a' Mhadaidh

Glenan Bay

Eilean a'Bhuic

To Tarbert

Loch Fyne

# GLENAN BAY

Some say that Glenan's last inhabitant walked out around the turn of the century. Others say that, maybe out of loneliness or despair, he hanged himself from an oak tree nearby. Today you would never guess Glenan had ever existed, tucked away as it is in rolling countryside between Tighnabruaich and Portavadie. The only reference on current maps to its name is nearby Glenan Bay, which looks west towards Tarbert on Loch Fyne.

But if you look closely at a large-scale map you will see tiny rectangles denoting buildings. Seek out the spot where those rectangles are supposed to be and you will indeed find traces of buildings. But now they are the ruins of cottages and steadings which once made up a settlement that lasted from 1309 until well after the Clearances had destroyed other Highland communities. Glenan, now known as the deserted village, is a poignant feature of a walk in an area rich in scenery and good walking routes.

This walk is on land bought by the Forestry Commission in 1961. The Commission planted conifers on about 45 hectares, but these were cleared about 25 years later following a study of native woodlands in Cowal. The study revealed the importance of the oak woodland at Glenan Bay, both in its own right and as a habitat for a wide variety of wildlife. One prized inhabitant of what is now the 140-hectare Glenan Forest Nature Reserve is the nightjar. The reserve is one of the few nesting sites in Scotland for this long-tailed insectivore, which makes itself known by a nocturnal *churring* song.

The walk begins at the reserve's car park and picnic area, near the Portavadie-Tarbert ferry

## INFORMATION

**Distance:** 5.5km (3.5 miles).

**Start and finish:** Forestry Commission car park and picnic site, Glenan Bay.

**Terrain:** Good woodland paths along most of route. A small unbridged burn has to be crossed. Headland has difficult, rocky, heather-covered ground. Wellingtons essential after rain.

**Public transport:** Limited Stagecoach Western Scottish bus service from Portavadie to Tighnabruaich, with connections to Dunoon.

**Refreshments:** None on route. restaurants and hotels at Kames and Tighnabruaich.

Ruins of the deserted village.

Waves wash spume
ashore at Glenan Bay.

terminal. From the picnic area, follow the track towards the shore then into the wood. You soon reach two signposts which indicate the Glenan Bay Shore Path and Glenan Bay Forest Path. Turn right up the forest path, which rises gradually through the oakwood. Here the trees are relatively short and contorted, creating an eerie, almost 'witchwood' atmosphere. Vigorous attempts have been made to slash back the bracken.

Continue past young broadleaved trees planted in plastic tubes to speed up growth and protect them from weather and animals. When you see the bay ahead, you find two more signs for the bay and forest walks. Opposite the signs, follow a track leading inland, marked by white posts. This track, very wet after rain, goes through reeds and bracken into an oakwood of bigger trees. It is was in this beautiful spot, so the story goes, that the man hanged himself.

Continue under the archway of a fallen but still living oak, then down a bracken-covered slope to a stream. Cross the stream easily by stones then climb up the opposite bank until you reach Glenan. There is nothing to warn you of what to expect: suddenly, as you mount the hill, stone walls and gable ends rise out of the shoulder-high bracken.

It is hard to make out the number of buildings in Glenan, but at least six can be counted from a rocky hillock overlooking the site. Bracken and rowan trees have invaded the area so thoroughly that you have to watch your step as you walk over tumbled-down boulders. Through what remains of one gable-end window, you can see across Loch Fyne to Kintyre. These cottages were once the homes of people who made, it seems, a reasonable living from the land.

About 300 years ago, three people had a large enough income to qualify for the two shillings hearth tax.

They were Gilbryde McMillan, John McConnichie and Ewan McConnichie. In 1758 a Robert McConnichie made a down payment of four guineas and paid £9 rent as well as payment in kind to rent land at Glenan from the Lamont chief. So life need not have been desperate at Glenan, especially if your name was McConnichie.

The path to Glenan disappears into a plantation, heading north towards the Kilfinan-Millhouse road. Return to the main path and turn right down to Glenan Bay, a long arc of shingle backed by machair and sandy pasture, with the island of Eilean a' Bhuic at its entrance. Follow a path through the machair to a burn with stepping stones. Even after heavy rain this burn is safe to cross, but wellingtons are then essential and a stick is handy for balance.

Soon after the burn, the path goes over a rocky shoulder, with an easy scramble down its far side. The path briefly disappears before guiding you through another notch in a rocky outcrop. It then leads across the neck of the headland to the southern end of the neighbouring bay, where attractive picnic spots can be found.

At the northern point of Glenan Bay, looking to Eilan a'Bhuic.

It is worth walking along the headland to see waves rushing through the gap between the point and the island. The terrain is difficult, especially for children, as the headland is covered with thigh-high heather and scored by rocky gullies. A relatively easy way along the headland is above the Glenan Bay shoreline.

The return route leads back round the bay to where the shore path came down to the shingle. Continue south along the shore path and cross a narrow neck of land to enter a grove of oaks. The path leads through the trees and bouldery outcrops, eventually passing the junction where you turned right up the forest path.

On the last stretch back to the picnic site, you may see the ferry setting off to or returning from Tarbert.

Kilometres 0 _____ 1
Miles 0 _____ 0.5

Path to Glenan Bay

P

To Tighnabruaich

Pier

**Portavadie**

To Tarbert

*Port a'
Mhadaidh*

**Pollphail
Village**

Start/Finish

Stillaig
Farm

**Standing
Stones**

**Standing
Stone**

**Low
Stillaig**

*Port Leathan*

*Asgog Bay*

*Salann Bay*

*Eilean Aoidhe*

N

*Sgat Mor*

*Loch Fyne*

# PORTAVADIE AND LOW STILLAIG

I t leans drunkenly, like a concrete lamp-post hit by a stolen car. Some 9ft (2.75m) tall, it dwarfs its neighbour, a low stump of stone about the size of a beer keg. They've been together a long time, an odd couple lasting out the centuries above Loch Fyne, near Ardlamont Point on the Cowal Peninsula. These standing stones from the Bronze Age (2,300-700BC) are on a right of way which forms part of this short but fascinating walk.

The story behind the stones may never be known for certain. But before we speculate from lofty hindsight about 'primitive superstition', we should take note of something at the start of the walk.

The walk begins at Portavadie, a short distance west of Kames and Tighnabruaich. This tiny community made barely a ripple on the surface of Loch Fyne or in the media until 1975 when the Government bought land to build an oil construction yard. The site had one big virtue, access to deep water, but it was at the end of a single-track road and had no large pool of local labour.

The site was intended to build concrete oil production platforms for the North Sea. The facts that Portavadie was on the opposite side of the country, and oil companies preferred steel platforms, were apparently irrelevant. Over £11 million was spent on building a workers' village, Pollphail, and digging out a dry dock. Nothing happened. The yard didn't win an order and the dry dock was dubbed the most expensive hole in Europe.

The workers' accommodation blocks rot to this day, still covering the original 100m start to the right of way. The walk now begins further from the shore, to the

## INFORMATION

**Distance:** 5km (3.1 miles).

**Start and Finish:** Outside the main gate of Pollphail workers' village, Portavadie.

**Terrain:** Mixture of moorland covered in heather and bracken, and good farm road. Waterproof footwear advised for boggy stretches after rain.

**Public transport:** Stagecoach Western Scottish buses from Portavadie to Tighnabruaich, and connections to Dunoon.

**Refreshments:** None on route. Hotels and restaurants at Kames and Tighnabruaich.

Standing stone at Low Stillaig.

left of the blocks, and is identified by a Scottish Rights
of Way Society sign. The route crosses reedy, wet
ground to a fence, and then goes along an often muddy

Overlooking site of the
never used oil production
platform yard at
Portavadie.

sheep walk through gorse bushes and young trees to a
heather-covered ridge overlooking Pollphail.

Local people have ignored this start because the blocks
affected drainage. The route taken is now apparently
through a break in the fence right of the entrance gate.
Then follow a concrete road for about 100m past the
blocks, climb a low grassy bank and cross a fence
where a white metal pipe has been driven into the
ground.

There is no longer a clear path down to the now-
unoccupied farm of Low Stillaig, and much of the
lower ground is covered in bracken. Nevertheless, the
route is straightforward.

Head up through silver birch to the top of the ridge.
From here you get an outstanding view west to the
town of Tarbert and the eastern shore of Kintyre.
Tarbert stands on an isthmus only 1km wide. In 1093,
Magnus Barefoot, King of Norway, claimed Kintyre
after he crossed the isthmus in a galley dragged by his
men. His claim was based on an agreement with King
Malcolm III of Scotland that he could control all the
land he could sail round.

Descend the ridge then head south, soon passing through a small enclosure surrounded by a low wall. Continue south until you see the two standing stones, about 200m uphill from a lorry's rusting hulk. Alternatively, you can avoid the bracken by moving over to the right of the enclosure to follow the bracken's edge, high above the shoreline, before swinging left towards the stones.

Elizabeth B. Rennie in her fascinating book *Cowal, A Historical Guide* (published by Birlinn) says that one theory for the stones' existence was that they and a third stone, 500m southeast, might have been used to study the moon's movements, possibly to time crop planting and other farming activities. Whatever their purpose, they now create a haunting scene in a beautiful landscape.

The island of Arran can be seen to the south as you continue to Low Stillaig, where you turn east to the narrow neck of land separating the little bays of Port Leathan and Salann. A popular picnic spot, Asgog Bay, is tucked round the corner from Salann Bay. At Salann are huts used by the Boys Brigade, who lease this area from the local landowner, farmer Calum Millar.

Mr Millar has kindly agreed that the farm road leading north to the Portavadie road can be used by walkers. A short distance up this road is the third standing stone, mentioned earlier. Further on, the road overlooks Mr Millar's home, Stillaig Farm. It was here in 1749, a time when smuggling was rife, that two kegs of spirits were found hidden in a barn.

The road back from Salann Bay.

Returning to the narrow main road, turn left and return to Portavadie. Watch out for traffic shortly before every hour. It is coming to and from the Tarbert-Portavadie ferry.

# INDEX

Other titles in this series

25 Walks – In and Around Aberdeen
25 Walks – In and Around Belfast
25 Walks – The Chilterns
25 Walks – The Cotswolds
25 Walks – Deeside
25 Walks – Dumfries and Galloway
25 Walks – Edinburgh and Lothian
25 Walks – Fife
25 Walks – In and Around Glasgow
25 Walks – Highland Perthshire
25 Walks – The Scottish Borders
25 Walks – The Trossachs
25 Walks – The Western Isles
25 Walks – The Yorkshire  Dales
25 Walks – In and Around London


Other titles in preparation

25 Walks – Down
25 Walks – Fermanagh
25 Walks – Skye and Kintail


Long distance guides published by The Stationery Office

The West Highland Way – Official Guide
The Southern Upland Way – Official Guide

**Published by The Stationery Office and available from:**

**The Stationery Office Bookshops**
71 Lothian Road, Edinburgh EH3 9AZ
(counter service only)
South Gyle Crescent, Edinburgh EH12 9EB
(mail, fax and telephone orders only)
0131-479 3141 Fax 0131-479 3142
49 High Holborn, London WC1V 6HB
(counter service and fax orders only)
Fax 0171-831 1326
68-69 Bull Street, Birmingham B4 6AD
0121-236 9696 Fax 0121-236 9699
33 Wine Street, Bristol BS1 2BQ
0117-926 4306 Fax 0117-929 4515
9-21 Princess Street, Manchester M60 8AS
0161-834 7201 Fax 0161-833 0634
16 Arthur Street, Belfast BT1 4GD
01232 238451 Fax 01232 235401
The Stationery Office Oriel Bookshop
The Friary, Cardiff CF1 4AA
01222 395548 Fax 01222 384347

**The Stationery Office publications are also available from:**

**The Publications Centre**
(mail, telephone and fax orders only)
PO Box 276, London SW8 5DT
General enquiries 0171-873 0011
Telephone orders 0171-873 9090
Fax orders 0171-873 8200

**Accredited Agents**
(see Yellow Pages)

*and through good booksellers*

Printed in Scotland for The Stationery Office by CCNo 70343 50c 4/97